Higher

History

Leckie×Leckie

First exam published in 2005.
Published by Leckie & Leckie Ltd, 3rd Floor, 4 Queen Street, Edinburgh EH2 1JE
tel: 0131 220 6831 fax: 0131 225 9987 enquiries@leckieandleckie.co.uk www.leckieandleckie.co.uk

ISBN 978-1-84372-680-7

A CIP Catalogue record for this book is available from the British Library.

Leckie & Leckie is a division of Huveaux plc.

Leckie & Leckie is grateful to the copyright holders, as credited at the back of the book, for permission to use their material.
Every effort has been made to trace the copyright holders and to obtain their permission for the use of copyright material.
Leckie & Leckie will gladly receive information enabling them to rectify any error or omission in subsequent editions.

[BLANK PAGE]

X044/301

NATIONAL QUALIFICATIONS 2005	MONDAY, 23 MAY 9.00 AM – 10.20 AM	**HISTORY HIGHER** Paper 1

Answer questions on **one** Option only.

Take particular care to show clearly the Option chosen. On the **front** of the answer book, **in the top right-hand corner**, write A or B or C.

Within the Option chosen, answer **two** questions, one from Historical Study: Scottish and British and one from Historical Study: European and World.

All questions are assigned 25 marks.

Marks may be deducted for bad spelling and bad punctuation, and for writing that is difficult to read.

SCOTTISH
QUALIFICATIONS
AUTHORITY

©

[BLANK PAGE]

OPTION A: MEDIEVAL HISTORY

Answer TWO questions, one from Historical Study: Scottish and British and one from Historical Study: European and World

Historical Study: Scottish and British

Medieval Society

1. To what extent was knight service the main characteristic of twelfth-century feudalism?

2. How far do you agree that the secular Church was more important to ordinary people than the regular Church?

3. "The influence of monarchs was the most important reason for the growth of towns in the twelfth century." Discuss.

4. To what extent was David I successful in establishing his authority over Scotland?

5. How far can it be argued that Henry II reformed the justice system in England to strengthen the power of the crown at the expense of the barons?

Historical Study: European and World

EITHER

Nation and King

6. How accurate is it to describe King John of England as a victim of circumstances?

7. Do you agree that Philip II's success can mainly be attributed to his belief that he should be "no man's vassal"?

8. To what extent was Louis IX responsible for the creation of a united French kingdom?

9. "The Scots could not have won the Wars of Independence without Robert Bruce." Discuss.

OR

Crisis of Authority

10. To what extent was French weakness the main reason for English success in the Hundred Years' War up to 1421?

11. How significant an impact did the Hundred Years' War have on France and England?

12. Assess the impact of the Black Death on England, Scotland and continental Europe.

13. How far was the Avignon Papacy responsible for the problems which faced the Church in the fourteenth and fifteenth centuries?

[Turn over

OPTION B: EARLY MODERN HISTORY

Answer TWO questions, one from Historical Study: Scottish and British and one from Historical Study: European and World

Historical Study: Scottish and British

EITHER

Scotland in the Age of the Reformation 1542–1603

1. To what extent did the "rough wooing" force the Scots to adopt a pro-French policy by 1548?

2. Explain the success of the Protestant Reformation in 1560.

3. "Mary ultimately lost the throne not because of her loyalty to Rome but because she entered into a scandalous marriage." How far do you agree?

4. How successful was James VI as king of Scotland before 1603?

5. To what extent was the Reformation of 1560 a significant turning point in Scottish history?

OR

Scotland and England in the Century of Revolutions 1603–1702

6. How far would you agree that the Union of Crowns brought no real advantages to Scotland?

7. Explain the rise of the Covenanter movement in Scotland.

8. "Charles I's obsession with authority and control was the main cause of the English Civil War." Do you agree?

9. Do you agree that the Protectorate offered no more than "a return to old forms of government under new management"?

10. To what extent did the Glorious Revolution settle the issues in the struggles between King and Parliament in the seventeenth century?

Historical Study: European and World

EITHER

Royal Authority in 17th and 18th Century Europe

11. How important was the nobility to the absolute government of Louis XIV?

12. "Of all Louis XIV's domestic policies, it was in religion that he had the least success." How far do you agree?

13. How successful was Frederick II of Prussia as an Enlightened Despot?

14. "Joseph II did little to solve the real problems of the Austrian people." Do you agree?

OR

The French Revolution: The Emergence of the Citizen State

15. How far do you agree that economic problems were the main threat to the stability of the Ancien Régime?

16. Why did the events of 1787–1789 result in revolution?

17. How far was Louis XVI responsible for his own execution?

18. To what extent did France become impossible to govern in the 1790s?

[Turn over

OPTION C: LATER MODERN HISTORY

Answer TWO questions, one from Historical Study: Scottish and British and one from Historical Study: European and World

Historical Study: Scottish and British

Britain 1850s–1979

1. Explain why Parliament gave the right to vote to increasing numbers of people between 1867 and 1928.

2. How far were the reports on poverty produced by Booth and Rowntree responsible for the Liberal social reforms of 1906–1914?

3. To what extent would you agree that the importance of the Suffragettes in gaining votes for women has been exaggerated?

4. How serious an impact did the Great Depression of the 1930s have on Britain?

5. How successful were the social reforms introduced by the Labour Government of 1945–1951?

Historical Study: European and World

EITHER

The Growth of Nationalism

6. How effectively did nationalists promote their cause in **either** Germany **or** Italy between 1815 and 1850?

7. **Either**

   (a) How important was the Zollverein in the achievement of national unification in Germany?

   Or

   (b) Evaluate the contribution of Garibaldi to national unification in Italy.

8. "Between 1871 and 1914 the new nation state attracted little popular support." How far would you agree with reference to **either** Germany **or** Italy during this period?

9. **Either**

   (a) To what extent were economic crises responsible for allowing the Nazis to achieve power in Germany in 1933?

   Or

   (b) "The breakdown of effective parliamentary government in Italy was the major factor in the Fascist rise to power." Discuss.

OR

The Large Scale State

The USA

10. Why did hostility towards immigration become a more serious issue in the USA after 1918?

11. "The business of America is business" (President Coolidge). How accurately does this describe the economic policies of Republican governments during the 1920s?

12. To what extent was the recovery of the USA from the Depression of the 1930s due to the New Deal?

13. To what extent was the growth of black radical movements in the 1960s due to the social and economic problems faced by black Americans in the cities of the North and West?

Russia

14. "Their threats to Tsarism were ineffective and disorganised." Discuss this view of the revolutionary movements in the years up to 1905.

15. "A direct result of Tsarist incompetence and blundering." How far do you agree with this view of the outbreak of the 1905 revolution?

16. Explain why the Provisional Government lost control of Russia in 1917.

17. To what extent was the Bolshevik victory in the Civil War due to Trotsky's skills as a military leader?

[END OF QUESTION PAPER]

[BLANK PAGE]

X044/302

NATIONAL
QUALIFICATIONS
2005

MONDAY, 23 MAY
10.40 AM – 12.05 PM

HISTORY
HIGHER
Paper 2

Answer questions on only **one** Special Topic.

Take particular care to show clearly the Special Topic chosen. On the **front** of the answer book, **in the top right-hand corner**, write the number of the Special Topic.

You are expected to use background knowledge appropriately in answering source-based questions.

Marks may be deducted for bad spelling and bad punctuation, and for writing that is difficult to read.

Some sources have been adapted or translated.

SCOTTISH
QUALIFICATIONS
AUTHORITY

©

[BLANK PAGE]

OPTION A: MEDIEVAL HISTORY

SPECIAL TOPIC 1: NORMAN CONQUEST AND EXPANSION 1050–1153

Study the sources below and then answer the questions which follow.

Source A: from G. O. Sayles, *The Medieval Foundations of England* (1966).

In the eyes of the English the successor to the throne was obvious, for at home Harold's claims were quite undisputed. He was the brother-in-law of the late king and, though this was not a blood relationship with the royal house of Wessex, yet the royal blood of the Danish dynasty ran in his veins. Furthermore, there is really good authority for his assertion that Edward had on his death bed named him as his heir. The wishes of a reigning monarch had much to do in deciding a successor . . . And for twelve years Harold had been the real protector and ruler of the kingdom and had proved his strength of character, his abilities as a statesman and his appreciation of the true line of English traditions . . .

William had little he could say on his own behalf. He was a cousin of the Confessor, but this relationship arose from marriage connections only and this had never been used in England as the basis of a claim to kingship.

William stressed the fact that in 1064 Harold had bound himself to him by an oath when the accident of a shipwreck had placed him in the hands of the Norman duke. What kind of oath it was we do not know: English writers say nothing about it, Norman writers say too much and most of it contradictory.

Source B: from M. Chibnall, *The Debate on the Norman Conquest* (1999).

When King Edward the Confessor died childless on 5 January 1066, he left no clear successor, and there were any number of possible claimants . . . The two strongest contenders were the man on the spot, Harold Godwinson, earl of Wessex, and William, duke of Normandy. Harold could offer no more than an extremely dubious claim to kinship; but he was the wealthiest and most powerful of the earls and the brother of King Edward's wife Edith . . .

When Cnut's direct line died out in 1042, Edward returned to England with some Norman backing, and it was widely believed in Normandy that he had named Duke William as his heir. So contradictory claims existed in England and Normandy before 1066.

The Normans increased their claim in 1064, when Harold Godwinson, on a mission to Normandy . . . was shipwrecked off the coast of Ponthieu, taken prisoner by Count Guy, and released only through the intervention of Duke William. The Normans alleged that he had voluntarily become William's vassal and had taken a solemn oath on relics to further his succession.

Source C: from the *Ecclesiastical History* of Orderic Vitalis, written *c.* 1114–1141.

Then Earl Copsi, the sons of Aethelgar, grandsons of King Edward, and many other men of wealth and high birth made their peace with William, and were allowed to keep all their possessions honourably when they had sworn fealty. The king went on from there to other parts of his kingdom, and everywhere arranged affairs to the advantage of the inhabitants as well as of himself. He appointed strong men from his Norman forces as guardians of the castles, and distributed rich fiefs that induced men to endure toil and danger to defend them.

Source D: from the *Ecclesiastical History* of Orderic Vitalis, written *c.* 1114–1141.

King William was justly renowned for his reforming zeal. In particular he loved true religion in churchmen for on this the peace and prosperity of the world depend . . . For when a bishop or abbot had come to the end of his life and died . . . the wise king appointed as bishop or abbot whoever seemed to his highest counsellors specially distinguished in life and doctrine. He followed this course for the fifty-six years that he ruled the duchy of Normandy and kingdom of England, so leaving a pious precedent for others to follow. Simony* was detestable to him, and so in appointing abbots or bishops he gave less weight to wealth and power than to wisdom and a good life. He appointed abbots of known virtue to the English monasteries, so that by their zeal and discipline monasticism, which had for a time been lax and faltering, revived and was restored to its former strength.

* Simony — paying money to be appointed to a church post.

Source E: from the speech of Robert Bruce (I) to David I at the Battle of the Standard, from *The Standard*, written by Ailred, abbot of Rievaulx in Yorkshire, in the mid twelfth century.

Against whom do you bear arms today and lead this huge army? Against the English, truly, and the Normans. O king, these are the men who have always given you useful counsel and ready help, and willing obedience besides.

Now you seek to destroy those through whom the kingdom was obtained for you. Who but our army restored Edgar, your brother, to the kingdom? You yourself, O king, when you demanded from your brother Alexander the part of the kingdom which Edgar had left to you at his death, obtained it without bloodshed through the fear of us.

[END OF SOURCES FOR SPECIAL TOPIC 1]

SPECIAL TOPIC 1: NORMAN CONQUEST AND EXPANSION 1050–1153

Answer *all* of the following questions.

Marks

1. Compare the views of Sayles (**Source A**) and Chibnall (**Source B**) about the rival claimants to the throne in 1066.
   Compare the sources overall and in detail. **4**

2. How fully does **Source C** explain the ways in which William established his control in England?
   Use the source and recalled knowledge. **6**

3. Is there sufficient evidence in **Source D** to argue that William reformed the Church in England?
   Use the source and recalled knowledge. **7**

4. How reliable is **Source E** as an explanation of why David I brought Anglo-Norman barons to Scotland?
   In reaching a conclusion you should refer to:
   * *the origin and possible purpose of the source;*
   * *the content of the source;*
   * *recalled knowledge.* **5**

5. To what extent was there a Norman achievement in Europe?
   *Use **Sources C, D** and **E** and recalled knowledge.* **8**

   (30)

[END OF QUESTIONS ON SPECIAL TOPIC 1]

SPECIAL TOPIC 2: THE CRUSADES 1096–1204

Study the sources below and then answer the questions which follow.

Source A: from a history of the First Crusade by the German monk Ekkehard, written *c.* 1101.

After Urban had aroused the spirits of all by the promise of forgiveness to those who undertook the crusade with single-hearted devotion, almost one hundred thousand men were appointed to the immediate service of God. They came from Aquitaine and Normandy, England, Scotland, Ireland, Brittany, Galicia, Gascony, France, Flanders, Lorraine, and from other Christian peoples, whose names I no longer retain. It was truly an army of "crusaders", for they bore the sign of the cross on their garments as a reminder that they should mortify the flesh, and in the hope that they would in this way triumph over the enemies of the cross of Christ. Thus, through the marvellous working of God's will, all these members of Christ, so different in speech, origin and nationality, were suddenly brought together as one body through their love of Christ.

Source B: from the *History of the Franks who captured Jerusalem*, by Raymond d'Aguilers, written in 1101.

And so, as we said, when our men were in a panic and while they were on the verge of despair, divine mercy was at hand for them . . . Thus, when the city of Antioch had been captured, the Lord, employing His power and kindness, chose a certain poor peasant through whom He comforted us . . . On that day, after the necessary preparations, and after every one had been sent out of the Church of St. Peter, twelve men, together with that man who had spoken of the Lance, began to dig . . . And after we had dug from morning to evening, some began to despair of finding the Lance . . . The youth who had spoken of the Lance, however, upon seeing us worn out, disrobed and, taking off his shoes, descended into the pit in his shirt, earnestly entreating us to pray to God to give us His Lance for the comfort and victory of His people. At length, the Lord was minded through the grace of His mercy to show us His Lance. And I, who have written this, kissed it when the point alone had as yet appeared above ground. What great joy then filled the city I cannot describe.

Source C: from Jonathan Riley-Smith, *The First Crusade and the Idea of Crusading* (1990).

The strangest of the discoveries was the Holy Lance which had pierced Christ's side during the crucifixion. A Southern French serving-man called Peter Bartholomew claimed to have had a vision of St. Andrew, who transported him into the church of St. Peter and produced the Holy Lance from a spot on the floor . . . There was . . . open scepticism, even hostility, shown by other leaders. There was, after all, a well known Holy Lance already in Constantinople. Adhemar of Le Puy's reaction was that of any good bishop to extraordinary claims and fervour; he openly expressed his doubts. So did Arnulf of Chocques and the bishop of Apt. Robert of Normandy, Robert of Flanders, Tancred and Bohemond were all very sceptical believing that Peter had simply brought a piece of iron with him into the cathedral.

Source D: from the *Alexiad* by Anna Comnena, written in 1140.

For he [Bohemond] was quick, and a man of very dishonest disposition. Although inferior to all the Latins who had crossed over into Asia, he was more malicious and courageous than any of them. But even though he thus excelled all in great cunning, the inconstant character of the Latins was also in him. Truly, the riches which he spurned at first, he now gladly accepted. For when this man of evil design had left his country in which he possessed no wealth at all (under the pretext, indeed, of adoring at the Lord's Sepulchre, but in reality trying to acquire for himself a kingdom), he found himself in need of much money, especially, indeed, if he was to seize the Roman power. In this he followed the advice of his father and, so to speak, was leaving no stone unturned.

Source E: from Christopher Tyerman, *The Invention of the Crusades* (1998).

As crusading became increasingly associated with papal wars in Italy in the fourteenth century, so there was a shift in criticism. Critics of wars within Christendom, even those under the guise of crusaders, persisted for as long as those wars continued . . . Advice presented to the Council of Lyon in 1274 had confirmed that there was hostility to political crusades and that a mixture of distraction, indifference and laziness stood in the path of new Holy Land Crusades. However, inertia and European wars, not the outcries of critics, crippled attempts by Gregory X to organise a new crusade.

[END OF SOURCES FOR SPECIAL TOPIC 2]

SPECIAL TOPIC 2: THE CRUSADES 1096–1204

Answer *all* of the following questions.

Marks

1. How valuable is **Source A** as evidence that religion was important in influencing people to go on crusade?
   In reaching a conclusion you should refer to:
   • *the origin and possible purpose of the source;*
   • *the content of the source;*
   • *recalled knowledge.*

   5

2. Compare the views expressed in **Sources B** and **C** about the discovery of the Holy Lance.
   Compare the sources overall and in detail.

   5

3. How well does **Source D** illustrate the character of Bohemond as a crusading leader?
   Use the source and recalled knowledge.

   6

4. How fully do **Sources A**, **B** and **D** demonstrate the motives of those who went on crusade?
   *Use **Sources A**, **B** and **D** and recalled knowledge.*

   8

5. How far does **Source E** describe the decline of the crusading ideal?
   Use the source and recalled knowledge.

   6

   (30)

[END OF QUESTIONS ON SPECIAL TOPIC 2]

OPTION B: EARLY MODERN HISTORY

SPECIAL TOPIC 3: SCOTLAND 1689–1715

Study the sources below and then answer the questions which follow.

Source A: from P. H. Scott, *Andrew Fletcher and the Treaty of Union* (1992).

It was the question of the succession to the throne which brought the relationship between the two countries to a critical point which had to be resolved one way or another. On 30 July 1700, William, duke of Gloucester, the last survivor of Queen Anne's eighteen children, died. There was no longer any obvious and automatic heir to the throne. The legitimate line of descent from James VII and II, the Jacobite Pretender, could not be re-established without overthrowing the Protestant settlement of the "Glorious Revolution". The English Parliament, again with no consultation with Scotland, in the Act of Succession of 1701, offered the throne to the Protestant Sophia, Electress of Hanover, and her descendants . . . The English Parliament seems to have assumed that Scotland would meekly accept their decision. In fact, their high-handed action called in question the survival of the union of the two monarchies which had come about in 1603. For all these reasons, the relationship with England reached a critical point in the early years of Anne's reign.

Source B: from a speech by Lord Belhaven on the first Article of the Treaty, 2 November 1706.

I shall remind this honourable House, that we are the successors of our noble forefathers, who founded our monarchy, framed our laws, without the assistance or advice of any foreign power or ruler; and who, during the time of two thousand years have handed them down to us, a free and independent nation . . . Shall we not then argue for that which our forefathers have purchased for us so dearly, and with so much immortal honour and glory? God forbid . . . if our descendants, after we are dead and gone, shall find themselves under an ill-made bargain . . . they will certainly say, "Ah! Our nation has been reduced to the last extremity at the time of this treaty; all our great men who in the past defended the rights and liberties of the nation, have all been killed and lie dead in the bed of honour, before ever the nation was reduced to agree to such contemptible terms . . . They have certainly all been extinguished, and now we are slaves for ever".

Source C: from George Lockhart of Carnwath, *Scotland's Ruine* (1714).

But the Equivalent was the mighty bait, for here with the sum of three hundred and ninety one thousand and eighty five pounds sterling to be sent in cash to Scotland. However, the Scots were to pay it and much more back again in a few years by agreeing to bear a share of the burdens imposed on England and used for payment of England's debts . . . This may chiefly explain why so many of them agreed to this union. The hopes of recovering what they had spent on the Company of Scotland, and of paying debts and arrears due to them . . . made many overlook the general interest of their country.

Source D: from Rosalind Mitchison, *Lordship to Patronage* (1983).

Enough of such a machinery already existed to smooth the conduct of affairs, yet in fact the distribution of honours and money on this occasion was small. Some peerages were given, and some payment of arrears and salary, amounting in all to £20,000, were secretly made. The sums were small even in the terms in which the parliamentary classes worked . . . Their smallness suggests that they really were arrears and not bribes. The main offer which the English dominated government could make to Scottish politicians was of course a share in power, and about this there were reservations not yet apparent . . .

It was still necessary to get the volatile Scottish Parliament to agree to the treaty. A vital step in the process was to be an Act assuring the Scottish Church establishment.

Source E: from an early eighteenth-century Jacobite song "Caledon, O Caledon how wretched is thy fate?"

> In Days of Yore you were renowned,
> Conspicuous was your fame,
> All nations did your Valour Praise,
> And Loyalty Proclaim;
>
> You did your Ancient Rights maintain,
> And Liberties defend,
> And scorned to have it thought that you
> On England did depend.
>
> Unto your Kings you did adhere,
> Stood by the Royal Race;
> With them you honour great did gain,
> And Paths of Glory trace;
> With Royal Stewart at your Head
> All enemies oppose,
> And like our brave Courageous Clans,
> In Pieces cut your foes . . .

[END OF SOURCES FOR SPECIAL TOPIC 3]

SPECIAL TOPIC 3: SCOTLAND 1689–1715

Answer *all* of the following questions.

Marks

1. To what extent does **Source A** explain why relations between Scotland and England became worse in the period 1690–1705?
   Use the source and recalled knowledge. **7**

2. How useful is **Source B** as evidence of opposition in Scotland towards the Union?
   In reaching a conclusion you should refer to:
   * *the origin and possible purpose of the source;*
   * *the content of the source;*
   * *recalled knowledge.* **5**

3. Compare the views expressed in **Sources C** and **D** on the importance of financial incentives in passing the Act of Union.
   Compare the sources overall and in detail. **4**

4. To what extent do **Sources A, C** and **D** explain why the Act of Union was passed?
   *Use **Sources A, C** and **D** and recalled knowledge.* **8**

5. How typical is **Source E** of the views of Scottish opponents of the Union in the period after 1707?
   Use the source and recalled knowledge. **6**

(30)

[END OF QUESTIONS ON SPECIAL TOPIC 3]

SPECIAL TOPIC 4: THE ATLANTIC SLAVE TRADE

Study the sources below and then answer the questions which follow.

Source A: from the evidence of Alexander Falconbridge, a surgeon who served on Slave ships, to a Parliamentary Committee, 1790.

The men Negroes, on being brought aboard ship, are immediately fastened together two and two, by handcuffs on their wrists, and by irons riveted on their legs . . . They are frequently stowed so close as to allow no other posture than lying on their sides. Neither will the height between the decks, unless directly under the grating, permit them to stand, especially where there are platforms, which is generally the case. These platforms are a kind of shelf, about eight or nine feet in breadth, extending from the side of the ship towards the centre. They are placed nearly midway between the decks, at the distance of two or three feet from each deck. Upon these the Negroes are stowed in the same manner as they are on the deck underneath.

Source B: "a black on yellow Jasper Slave Medallion made in the Etruria factory of Josiah Wedgwood in support of the anti-slavery campaign."

Source C: from Peter J. Kitson, *Slavery, Abolition and Emancipation: Volume 2 – The Abolition Debate* (1999).

Various arguments that circulated in support of the trade usually originated from the Society of West India Planters and the merchants of London, Bristol and Liverpool. This propaganda was financed by a levy on West Indian imports into the port of London and was strongly backed by the MPs. From the start there was little attempt at a moral justification of the trade . . . By and large the pro-slavery propagandists stressed the economic argument. While reform of the plantations was necessary, abolition would simply mean handing over the trade to competitor nations. A common argument was that in many ways the slaves were better off than the labouring poor in Britain. Slavery was defended as a necessary evil that had always existed. Jamaica and the other West Indian islands were not able to sustain an increasing slave population and therefore relied on the trade for essential labour.

Source D: from Samuel Taylor Coleridge, *On the Slave Trade* (1796).

It has been asserted by more than one writer on the subject that the plantation slaves are at least as well off as the peasantry in England. Now I appeal to common sense, whether to affirm that the slaves are as well off as our peasantry is not the same as to assert that our peasantry are as badly off as Negro slaves? And whether if our peasantry believed it, they would not be inclined to rebel?

[It is said] that the slaves are more humanely treated and live more happily in the plantations than in their native country. If any person should entertain a doubt of this, the slave-merchants, slave-holders, and slave-drivers together with the manufacturers of neck-collars and thumbscrews, are ready and willing to take their bible oaths on it! When treated with tolerable humanity the human race, as well as other animals, multiplies. The Negroes multiply in their native country: they do *not* multiply in the West Indian islands; for if they did, the slave trade would have been abolished long ago by its lack of usefulness.

Source E: from James Walvin, "Public Campaign in England", in D. Eltis and J. Walvin (eds), *The Abolition of the Atlantic Slave Trade* (1981).

The emergence of popular radicalism (English Jacobinism to its enemies) . . . transformed the political climate in England. War with France in 1793, and the disintegration in Haiti (with the loss of thousands of British troops in a forlorn campaign against former slaves in that island), did nothing to help the abolitionist cause . . . Popular associations, petitions, cheap publications, public lectures, large public meetings, pressure on Parliament: these, the lifeblood of abolitionism, were now adopted by the radicals. And in the process these came to be resisted as a potentially disastrous repeat of events in France.

[END OF SOURCES FOR SPECIAL TOPIC 4]

SPECIAL TOPIC 4: THE ATLANTIC SLAVE TRADE

Answer *all* of the following questions.

Marks

1. How valuable is **Source A** as evidence of conditions on the Middle Passage?
   In reaching a conclusion you should refer to:
   * *the origin and possible purpose of the source;*
   * *the content of the source;*
   * *recalled knowledge.*

   5

2. How typical is **Source B** of the methods used by abolitionists?
   Use the source and recalled knowledge.

   6

3. To what extent does **Source C** identify the arguments used by supporters of the Slave Trade?
   Use the source and recalled knowledge.

   6

4. How far does **Source D** support the pro-slavery arguments outlined in **Source C**?
   Compare the sources overall and in detail.

   5

5. How fully do **Sources C, D** and **E** explain the difficulties faced by abolitionists in their campaign?
   *Use **Sources C, D and E** and recalled knowledge.*

   8

   (30)

[END OF QUESTIONS ON SPECIAL TOPIC 4]

SPECIAL TOPIC 5: THE AMERICAN REVOLUTION

Study the sources below and then answer the questions which follow.

Source A: from a letter from Joseph Reed of Philadelphia to the earl of Dartmouth, American Secretary, June 1774.

I cannot think myself a rebel or a traitor. I love my king, respect the Parliament, and have the highest regard for the mother country, and these are the sentiments of every important person with whom I speak . . . But if the Port of Boston Bill and the other proceedings against that province have been founded on a supposition that the other colonies would leave them to struggle alone, I do assure your Lordship there never was a greater mistake.

Source B: from a speech in Parliament by Lord North on the Port of Boston Bill, 1774.

We are now disputing, not I trust with all the Colonies, but with those who have maintained that we have as a Parliament no legislative right over them and that we are two independent states under the same king . . . We are not entering into a dispute between internal and external taxes, not between taxes levied for the purposes of revenue and taxes levied for the regulation of trade, not between representation and taxation, or legislation and taxation. But we are now to dispute the question whether we have or have not any authority in that country.

Source C: from Peter D. G. Thomas, *Revolution in America* (1992).

The root cause of the American Revolution was the question of whether or not Parliament was the legislature for the British Empire. Public discussion of the constitutional relationship between Britain and her colonies was stimulated from 1763 because government measures increasingly took the form of Parliamentary legislation instead of executive action by the Crown. Parliamentary sovereignty over Britain's overseas possessions had been assumed rather than frequently exercised or asserted. The colonial challenge during the Stamp Act Crisis led to the Declaratory Act of 1766, the first formal claim of full Parliamentary power over the Colonies. It took some time for the colonists to dispute this outright . . . The first practical exertion of complete Parliamentary power occurred with the legislation of 1774. That led to a direct colonial challenge to Parliament's power of legislation. It was an implicit demand for internal home rule under the Crown, and a claim quite incompatible with the greatest concession any British politician would make.

Source D: from Ray Raphael, *The American Revolution, A People's History* (2001).

On May 31, 1774, Philip Vickers Fithian from the Northern Neck of Virginia recorded in his journal: "The lower class of people here are agitated by the account of reports from Boston, many of them expect to be pressed and compelled to go and fight the British!" Not that these common folk were unpatriotic: when the alarm sounded a year later, they joined companies of volunteers in great numbers. But they didn't want to be forced into service. They didn't want to leave their homes for extended periods of time, nor to take orders from men who claimed to be their superiors.

In the spring and summer of 1775, during the height of the military fever, plain farmers from Virginia seized control of the volunteer companies which had originally been formed by gentry . . . They insisted on voting for their own officers. As volunteers, they also insisted on the right to come or leave as they pleased.

Source E: from "Derry Down", a British song from the time of the American Revolution.

America . . .
Now finds she's being used by both France and Spain,
Yet all three united can't weigh down the scale,
So the Dutchman jumps in with the hope to prevail.
Derry down, down, down, derry down
Yet Britain will boldly their efforts withstand,
And bravely defy them by sea and by land.

[END OF SOURCES FOR SPECIAL TOPIC 5]

SPECIAL TOPIC 5: THE AMERICAN REVOLUTION

Answer *all* of the following questions.

Marks

1. How valuable is **Source A** as evidence of the colonists' attitude to Britain in the years before the outbreak of war?
   In reaching a conclusion you should refer to:
   - *the origin and possible purpose of the source;*
   - *the content of the source;*
   - *recalled knowledge.*   **5**

2. To what extent does the evidence in **Source B** support the analysis in **Source C** of the nature of the dispute between Britain and the Colonies?
   Compare the sources overall and in detail.   **5**

3. How fully do **Sources A**, **B** and **C** reveal the reasons for the colonial challenge to British control in America?
   *Use **Sources A**, **B** and **C** and recalled knowledge.*   **8**

4. How important are the issues raised in **Source D** in understanding the problems faced by the Continental army after the outbreak of war?
   Use the source and recalled knowledge.   **6**

5. How accurately does **Source E** assess the significance of foreign intervention in the American War of Independence?
   Use the source and recalled knowledge.   **6**

    (30)

[END OF QUESTIONS ON SPECIAL TOPIC 5]

OPTION C: LATER MODERN HISTORY

SPECIAL TOPIC 6: PATTERNS OF MIGRATION: SCOTLAND 1830s–1930s

Study the sources below and then answer the questions which follow.

Source A: from a *Report on the Condition of the Poorer Classes of Edinburgh and their Dwellings, Neighbourhoods and Families* (1868).

In the Middle Meal Market Stairs are 59 rooms entered by a steep, dark, stone stair, common to all. In these dwell 248 individuals, divided into 56 families. And in these dens there is no water, no water-closet, no sink. The women living on the fifth or highest floor have to carry all their water up the close and up these stairs. It is not difficult to imagine the state of wet and filth in which they must continually be. In Birtley Buildings in the Canongate a similar picture exists. These are not exceptional cases; there are hundreds of others as bad; indeed, the census for 1861 brought out distinctly that in Edinburgh there were actually 13,209 families living in a single room, more than one third of our whole population. It appears that more than 900 of these were cellars, most of them damp and totally dark. It must not be supposed that these 13,209 families are the immoral and abject poor alone. Among them are to be found nearly all our common labouring classes, a great many of whom are of Irish stock.

Source B: from the report of the Education Commission (Scotland) (1866).

The people in the Clyde district are of the poorest classes and this district has a large mixture of Irish immigrants. For this large Irish element and their needs there exists no school within the district, beyond a private adventure school in one of the wynds. Roman Catholic children are indeed to be found in the other schools but in comparatively small numbers and their attendance is extremely irregular. It is a fact that many children in the Clyde district, both Catholic and Protestant, but chiefly the former, attend no school. What are these neglected children doing, then, if they are selling matches and running errands, cared for by no-one, not at school? They are idling in the streets and wynds, tumbling about in the gutters.

Source C: from W. Hamish Fraser and R. J. Morris (eds), *People and Society in Scotland Vol.II, 1830–1914* (1990).

The uneven pace of an industrialising and urbanising society was reflected in distinctive religious, cultural and educational divisions. The largest number of schools, pupils and teachers was to be found in Glasgow, but many of those were Catholic schools outside the state system. Irish settlement, especially after the Famine, produced an ever-growing demand for Catholic schools and teachers. Nonetheless, by the 1860s, the Catholic clergy could boast that they had overcome the immense difficulties and could offer pupils instruction in the three Rs and the Bible. But the community lacked the resources to pay adequate school fees or to raise the necessary funds towards teachers' salaries and school buildings. As a result, by the end of the century, there was a growing crisis in Catholic education.

Source D: from J. A. Jackson, *The Irish in Britain* (1963).

The success of the Irish settlement in Britain is concealed by placing undue emphasis on the problems with which the Irish have been associated and on the clashes of religion and temperament which have occurred between the immigrants and native population. The typical pattern of settlement, consolidation and gradual assimilation into the host community is told in the far less dramatic life history of individuals and families. Gradually the immigrant found his voice in the Press and in politics. He found and fought for his power in the labour movement; through benevolent societies he achieved economic security. He found comfort and support in the clubs and associations dedicated to his own culture.

Source E: from a letter from Michie Ewing from Canada to Colonel Charles Fraser, 1857.

It is now nearly two years since we left and God in his mercy has blessed us with remarkable good health in our adopted country. And although I have not been altogether so successful as I expected, yet I like the country, I like the climate and I am fully convinced that many a poor man would be much better here than in Scotland. Yet there are many who come here who would be much better at home than here. Wages are high, but much more work is expected and unless a man is a good workman few will employ him. A good many get disheartened and return home, go drinking or even lose their health and die. Yet, I have great cause to be thankful in that all the time I have had plenty of work and sometimes two or three persons wanting me at the one time.

[END OF SOURCES FOR SPECIAL TOPIC 6]

SPECIAL TOPIC 6: PATTERNS OF MIGRATION: SCOTLAND 1830s–1930s

Answer *all* of the following questions.

Marks

1. How useful is **Source A** as evidence of the living conditions experienced by Irish immigrants to Scotland?
   In reaching a conclusion you should refer to:
   * *the origin and possible purpose of the source;*
   * *the content of the source;*
   * *recalled knowledge.*
   5

2. Compare the views of **Sources B** and **C** concerning the provision of education for Irish immigrants to Scotland.
   Compare the sources overall and in detail.
   5

3. How successfully did other European immigrants preserve their identity in similar ways to the Irish as outlined in **Source D**?
   Use the source and recalled knowledge.
   6

4. Assess the impact of Irish immigrants on Scottish society between 1830 and 1930.
   *Use **Sources B**, **C** and **D** and recalled knowledge.*
   8

5. How typical of the experiences of emigrant Scots are those described in **Source E**?
   Use the source and recalled knowledge.
   6

   (30)

[END OF QUESTIONS ON SPECIAL TOPIC 6]

SPECIAL TOPIC 7: APPEASEMENT AND THE ROAD TO WAR, TO 1939

Study the sources below and then answer the questions which follow.

Source A: from minutes of a meeting of the British Cabinet, 11 March 1936.

From information given by the Service Ministers it is clear that our position at home and in home waters is a disadvantageous one whether from the point of view of the Navy, Army or Air Force or anti-aircraft defence. In addition, public opinion is strongly opposed to any military action against the Germans in the demilitarised zone. In particular, the ex-servicemen are very anti-French. Moreover, many people, perhaps most people, are openly saying that they do not see why the Germans should not reoccupy the Rhineland. In these circumstances it is generally accepted that it is worth taking almost any risk in order to escape from that situation.

Source B: a drawing from the *Illustrated London News*, published in 1937, showing ways in which the Royal Air Force was rearming as part of a five-year plan.

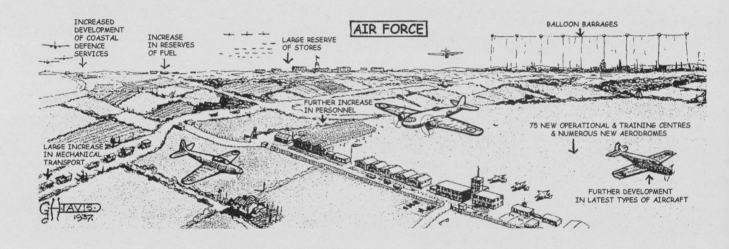

Source C: from the record kept by Dr. Kurt Schuschnigg, the Chancellor of Austria, of his meeting with Adolf Hitler, 12 February 1938.

Schuschnigg – Naturally, I realise that you can march into Austria, but . . . whether we wish it or not, that would lead to the shedding of blood. We are not alone in the world. That probably means war.

Hitler – Will you take the responsibility for that, Herr Schuschnigg? Don't believe that the world will hinder me in my decisions. Italy? I am quite clear with Mussolini; with Italy I am on the closest possible terms. England? England will not lift a finger for Austria . . . and France? Well, two years ago when we marched into the Rhineland with a handful of battalions—at that moment I risked a great deal. If France had marched then we should have been forced to withdraw . . . But for France it is now too late.

Source D: from the leading article, *Glasgow Herald*, 14 March 1938.

It is time for Britain's rulers to make up their minds clearly and unmistakably about the position we are ready to take up in Europe and the world. That is the plain message of what has happened in Austria. Europe is faced with a type of political leadership which will be bound by no ordinary promises, which is ready to use force to the utmost when the indecision or weakness of peacefully minded powers leaves the way to violence open. In this matter the rights and wrongs of the Anschluss itself are beside the point.

All that matters are the attitudes of Nazi Germany towards agreements freely made by its leaders and their lack of sincerity in dealing with friendly governments such as our own. In face of these things, are we to adopt the ideas of the isolationists, abandon all active interest in Europe and prepare to defend unaided our own territories and trade throughout all the world? Or are we to lay down the limit beyond which we shall not be prepared to allow the forcible remaking of Europe to proceed? No British government has made it clear either to ourselves or to the rest of the world just what we propose to do if France were to be drawn into a war by her continental alliances.

Source E: from Piers Brendon, *The Dark Valley* (2000).

With surprising speed a reaction set in against Munich. Feelings of joy at Britain's deliverance from war were overtaken by feelings of shame at the betrayal of Czechoslovakia. What had seemed a brave bid for peace in September appeared, as autumn progressed, to be a fatal act of cowardice in the face of alien strength. By 320 votes to 266 the Oxford Union carried a motion deploring "the Government's policy of peace with honour". On Bonfire Night . . . a "guy" was burned dressed in a black Homburg hat and a frock coat, complete with a neatly rolled umbrella. The government did badly in by-elections and china ornaments celebrating Chamberlain the peace-maker remained unsold in shops.

[END OF SOURCES FOR SPECIAL TOPIC 7]

SPECIAL TOPIC 7: APPEASEMENT AND THE ROAD TO WAR, TO 1939

Answer *all* of the following questions.

Marks

1. How fully does **Source A** explain the British reaction to the remilitarisation of the Rhineland?
   Use the source and recalled knowledge.

   6

2. Compare the evidence in **Sources A** and **B** about the condition of the British armed forces in the late 1930s.
   Compare the sources overall and in detail.

   5

3. How useful is **Source C** as evidence of Hitler's attitude towards Britain and France at the time of the Anschluss?
   In reaching a conclusion you should refer to:
   * *the origin and possible purpose of the source;*
   * *the content of the source;*
   * *recalled knowledge.*

   5

4. To what extent does **Source D** reflect British public opinion about the Anschluss?
   Use the source and recalled knowledge.

   6

5. How effective was the policy of appeasement in achieving its objectives?
   *Use **Sources C**, **D** and **E** and recalled knowledge.*

   8

   (30)

[END OF QUESTIONS ON SPECIAL TOPIC 7]

SPECIAL TOPIC 8: THE ORIGINS AND DEVELOPMENT OF THE COLD WAR 1945–1985

Study the sources below and then answer the questions which follow.

Source A: from a television broadcast by Walther Ulbricht, leader of the German Democratic Republic, 18 August 1961.

Eventful days lie behind us. The workers, and all the people of the German Democratic Republic, can breathe a sigh of relief . . . With growing anger, they had seen how they were being made fools of and robbed by the militarist rabble of the government in West Germany . . .

The Bonn government has rejected all our peaceful proposals. Their War Minister has ordered a speed-up in the atomic armament of their army, which is commanded by former Nazi generals . . .

We know their plans. They were aimed at creating conditions that would allow an open attack against the GDR and create civil war . . .

It was clear that a very dangerous situation had arisen for peace in Europe and the world. In order to remove this danger to the peace of our people and other peoples, we contacted our friends at an early date and agreed to take action against it.

Source B: from a statement to the West German Parliament by Konrad Adenauer, Chancellor of the Federal Republic of West Germany, 18 August 1961.

The Federal Government considers it essential to draw the attention of world public opinion to the true causes of this crisis . . .

It is not any militaristic or revenge-seeking policies by the Federal Government that have caused the rulers of the Soviet zone of Germany to take this action. It is the result of their refusal to let the people of the Soviet-occupied zone of Germany live according to the way of life which they desire . . .

The permanent flow of refugees in recent weeks tells a different story—the true story . . . In their desperation, they saw no other way out than to leave their homes in the Soviet-occupied zone . . . to begin a new life in freedom in the Federal Republic. There was nothing left for them but to "vote with their feet".

Source C: from J. Isaacs and T. Downing, *The Cold War* (1998).

When Nikita Khrushchev stood up to address the delegates of the Twenty Second Communist Party Congress in Moscow, he had something special to tell them . . . He announced that the Soviet Union had just detonated the largest bomb the world had ever seen—equivalent to more than 50 million tons of TNT . . . This heralded a new generation of Soviet superbombs.

Khrushchev told the party members that he hoped "we are never called upon to explode these bombs over anybody's territory". Khrushchev neatly summed up the Cold War's nuclear paradox. Each side devoted huge sums to developing weapons it hoped never to use.

Source D: from "What Lies Ahead", a newspaper article by Josef Smrkovsky, a leading supporter of the reform movement in Czechoslovakia, 9 February 1968.

The Central Committee of the party has attempted to find the cause of the tameness and indifference in our country . . . There is a conviction growing that there must be a basic change of course. Such a change must be aimed at the democratisation of the party and society as a whole . . . It must be backed by realistic guarantees that are understood by the majority of the people.

That is why the Central Committee has decided to draw up an Action Programme and start work on a project for the advancement of socialist society . . . We shall find no ready made solutions. It is up to us, both Czechs and Slovaks, to launch out into unexplored territory and search for a Czechoslovak road to socialism.

Source E: from a statement by the Central Committee of the Communist Party of the Soviet Union, 19 August 1968.

In recent days, events in Czechoslovakia have assumed a most ominous character . . . Right-wing forces have attempted to force the party and government of Czechoslovakia to follow a pro-Western policy and return Czechoslovakia to a bourgeois republic . . .

We have concluded that the moment has arrived to undertake active measures in defence of socialism in Czechoslovakia . . .

We have ordered our military units to take all necessary measures on 21 August to help the Czechoslovak working people in their struggle against reactionary forces and to protect their security against the intrigues of imperialism . . . Our enemies should be fully aware that no-one . . . will ever be permitted to break a single link in the community of socialist states.

[END OF SOURCES FOR SPECIAL TOPIC 8]

SPECIAL TOPIC 8: THE ORIGINS AND DEVELOPMENT OF THE COLD WAR 1945–1985

Answer *all* of the following questions.

Marks

1. How valuable is **Source A** as evidence of East Germany's attitude towards West Berlin at this time?
   In reaching a conclusion you should refer to:
   * *the origin and possible purpose of the source;*
   * *the content of the source;*
   * *recalled knowledge.*

   5

2. Compare the views of the Berlin Crisis of 1961 given in **Sources A** and **B**.
   Compare the sources overall and in detail.

   5

3. How far do you accept the views in **Source C** on the development of the nuclear arms race?
   Use the source and recalled knowledge.

   6

4. How fully does **Source D** illustrate the growing demand for reform in Czechoslovakia in the 1960s?
   Use the source and recalled knowledge.

   6

5. To what extent do **Sources A**, **C** and **E** explain the issues which divided the Superpowers during the Cold War?
   *Use **Sources A, C** and **E** and recalled knowledge.*

   8

   (30)

[END OF QUESTIONS ON SPECIAL TOPIC 8]

SPECIAL TOPIC 9: IRELAND 1900–1985: A DIVIDED IDENTITY

Study the sources below and then answer the questions which follow.

Source A: from a speech by Winston Churchill, a Government Minister, at Celtic Park Football Ground, Belfast, 8 February 1912.

I come to you on the eve of a Home Rule Bill. We intend to place before Parliament our plan for the better government of Ireland . . . We have consulted, and we shall consult fully, with the leaders of Irish public opinion, but the decision rests with us . . .

The bill which we shall introduce will be a bill of a British Government designed to smooth the path of the British Empire, and liberate new forces for its services . . . For more than twenty-five years, Home Rule has been the policy of the Liberal Party. Liberals have been taught to believe that the best solution of Irish difficulties lies in the establishment of an Irish Parliament with an Executive responsible to it.

Source B: a cartoon published in 1914, showing John Redmond.

Source C: from Robert Kee, *The Green Flag* (1972).

The speed with which the election of 1918 was called acted in Sinn Féin's favour . . . Very many soldiers had not received their postal voting papers . . . It seems probable that many of them would have voted for the old Nationalist Party, rather than for Sinn Féin, still thought of as pro-German . . .

Sinn Féin was also much favoured in the election by the greatly enlarged new register, which almost trebled the previous Irish electorate . . .

Another telling factor was that Sinn Féin already seemed to be the winning party. In 26 constituencies, the Nationalist Party could not even find a candidate . . . Probably what most Sinn Féin voters were voting for was simply the greatest measure of independence, without partition of the country, which Ireland could get. The one thing they were certainly not voting for was an attempt to win independence by force of arms or a campaign of terrorism.

Source D: from a press statement by Eamonn de Valera, June 1922.

English propaganda will strive to lay the blame for this war on Irishmen, but the world outside must not be deceived. England's threat of war alone is responsible for the present situation.

In face of England's threat of war, some of our countrymen yielded. The men who are now being attacked by the forces of the Provisional Government are those who refuse to obey the order to yield—preferring to die. They are the best and bravest of our nation, and would most loyally have obeyed the will of the Irish people freely expressed. They are not willing that Ireland's independence should be abandoned under the lash of a foreign government.

Source E: from notes made by Michael Collins, August 1922.

Our opponents claim to be opposing the National Government which they declare to have seized power illegally. In view of the elections, this is absurd . . . And what are they complaining of? . . . Simply that the Government refused to let authority be wrested from it by an armed minority . . . We saw them pursuing exactly the same course as the English Black and Tans . . .

There is no British Government any longer in Ireland. It is gone. It is no longer the enemy. We have now our own government, constitutionally elected, and it is the duty of every Irish man and woman to obey it. Anyone who fails to obey it is an enemy of the people and must expect to be treated as such.

[END OF SOURCES FOR SPECIAL TOPIC 9]

SPECIAL TOPIC 9: IRELAND 1900–1985: A DIVIDED IDENTITY

Answer *all* of the following questions.

Marks

1. How effective was the policy of Home Rule, as outlined in **Source A**, in addressing the concerns of the Irish people at the time?
   Use the source and recalled knowledge.   **6**

2. How useful is **Source B** as evidence of the difficulties in carrying out the policy of Home Rule?
   In reaching a conclusion you should refer to:
   * *the origin and possible purpose of the source;*
   * *the content of the source;*
   * *recalled knowledge.*   **5**

3. To what extent does **Source C** explain the reasons for the victory of Sinn Féin in the election of 1918?
   Use the source and recalled knowledge.   **6**

4. Compare the views in **Sources D** and **E** on the reasons for the outbreak of the Irish Civil War.
   Compare the sources overall and in detail.   **5**

5. How fully do **Sources B**, **C** and **E** illustrate the development of division and conflict in Ireland between 1912 and 1922?
   *Use **Sources B**, **C** and **E** and recalled knowledge.*   **8**

(30)

[END OF QUESTIONS ON SPECIAL TOPIC 9]

[END OF QUESTION PAPER]

[BLANK PAGE]

[BLANK PAGE]

X044/301

NATIONAL QUALIFICATIONS 2006	MONDAY, 22 MAY 9.00 AM – 10.20 AM	**HISTORY HIGHER** Paper 1

Answer questions on **one** Option only.

Take particular care to show clearly the Option chosen. On the **front** of the answer book, **in the top right-hand corner**, write A or B or C.

Within the Option chosen, answer **two** questions, one from Historical Study: Scottish and British and one from Historical Study: European and World.

All questions are assigned 25 marks.

Marks may be deducted for bad spelling and bad punctuation, and for writing that is difficult to read.

SCOTTISH QUALIFICATIONS AUTHORITY

[BLANK PAGE]

OPTION A: MEDIEVAL HISTORY

**Answer TWO questions, one from Historical Study: Scottish and British
and one from Historical Study: European and World**

Historical Study: Scottish and British

Medieval Society

1. How difficult were the lives of the peasants, both free and un-free, in twelfth-century Scotland and England?

2. "The medieval Church was interested mainly in secular power. Religion came a poor second." Discuss.

3. How far do you agree that towns were a vital part of medieval society?

4. To what extent was there a "Norman colonisation" of Scotland during the reign of David I?

5. Discuss the view that the quarrel between Henry II and Thomas Becket was nothing more than a clash of personalities.

Historical Study: European and World

EITHER

Nation and King

6. "It was King John's unpleasant personality that led to the baronial opposition and Magna Carta." How far do you agree with this statement?

7. To what extent was Philip II a successful monarch?

8. To what extent did a community of the realm develop in Scotland during the period 1286–1298?

9. How important was the Battle of Bannockburn in ensuring Scottish victory in the Wars of Independence?

OR

Crisis of Authority

10. "The Hundred Years' War was fought mainly to decide whether kings of England should still hold lands in France as vassals of the French king." Discuss.

11. To what extent was the poll tax of 1380 the major cause of the Peasants' Revolt of 1381?

12. Why was the Conciliar Movement (1409–1449) unable to solve fully the problems facing the Church at the start of the fifteenth century?

13. To what extent was there a crisis of authority in Europe in the fourteenth and fifteenth centuries?

OPTION B: EARLY MODERN HISTORY

Answer TWO questions, one from Historical Study: Scottish and British and one from Historical Study: European and World

Historical Study: Scottish and British

EITHER

Scotland in the Age of the Reformation 1542–1603

1. What was the most serious weakness of the Church before 1560?

2. To what extent did rivalry between England and France dominate Scottish politics between 1542 and 1560?

3. "Selfish and greedy nobles made Scotland impossible to rule." How important was this as a reason for Mary, Queen of Scots, losing her throne?

4. How important was the establishment of law and order to the success of James VI's reign in Scotland?

5. Do you consider that religious issues were the main cause of conflict in Scotland between 1542 and 1603?

OR

Scotland and England in the Century of Revolutions 1603–1702

6. "Financial issues caused the most serious challenges to the authority of James I in England after 1603." How far do you agree?

7. Why did Charles I find it so difficult to rule Scotland?

8. To what extent was religion the main cause of the Civil War in England?

9. Why did Cromwell fail to find an acceptable form of government for England in the 1650s?

10. "The Glorious Revolution was the climax to the Parliamentary challenge to royal authority in the seventeenth century." Discuss.

Historical Study: European and World

EITHER

Royal Authority in 17th and 18th Century Europe

11. How important was Louis XIV's personal role in the government of France?

12. "A disastrous failure." How accurate is this description of Louis XIV's treatment of religious minorities in France?

13. "Frederick II of Prussia was more interested in efficient government than in the welfare of his people." How far do you agree?

14. "Here lies a king who failed in all he tried to do." Was Joseph II fair to himself in writing this epitaph?

OR

The French Revolution: The Emergence of the Citizen State

15. To what extent were the grievances of the peasants a threat to the Ancien Régime?

16. Explain why the revolt of the nobles in 1787 resulted in violent revolution by 1789.

17. "The flight of Louis XVI to Varennes guaranteed the end of the monarchy." How far do you agree?

18. Why was there so much instability in France between 1793 and 1799?

[Turn over

OPTION C: LATER MODERN HISTORY

Answer TWO questions, one from Historical Study: Scottish and British and one from Historical Study: European and World

Historical Study: Scottish and British

Britain 1850s–1979

1. Discuss the view that by 1914 Britain was not yet a democratic country.

2. To what extent did the social reforms of the Liberal Government (1906–1914) improve the lives of the British people?

3. How important were socialist societies in the growth of the Labour Party by 1906?

4. "The National Government (1931–1940) has been criticised most unfairly for its economic policies." How far would you agree?

5. **Either**

   (*a*) To what extent did urbanisation benefit the people of Scotland during the period 1880–1939?

   Or

   (*b*) How far did varying levels of support for the Scottish National Party between 1945 and 1979 result from changes in the Scottish economy?

Historical Study: European and World

EITHER

The Growth of Nationalism

6. Why was unification achieved in Germany **or** Italy?

7. **Either**

   (a) To what extent was national unity a problem within Germany between 1871 and 1914?

   Or

   (b) What was the most serious difficulty the new Italian state faced between 1871 and 1914?

8. "Resentment towards the peace treaties at the end of the First World War made the rise of fascism inevitable." Discuss with reference to **either** Germany **or** Italy.

9. "Totalitarian rule benefited most of the people." Do you agree with this opinion about **either** Germany between 1933 and 1939 **or** Italy between 1922 and 1939?

OR

The Large Scale State

The USA

10. How important was the Ku Klux Klan in causing the problems facing black Americans during the 1920s and 1930s?

11. Why did some Americans not share in the general economic prosperity of the 1920s?

12. How effective were the increased powers of the federal government in dealing with the social and economic problems facing the USA in the 1930s?

13. "The experience of black American soldiers during the Second World War was the main cause of increased pressure for civil rights after 1945." How far do you agree?

Russia

14. How important was the policy of Russification in assisting the Tsarist state to maintain its authority in the years before 1905?

15. Why did the Dumas have so little influence on the Tsarist state between 1905 and 1914?

16. "Nicholas II's fall from power was due mainly to his own weaknesses as a ruler." How far do you accept this explanation for the Revolution of February 1917?

17. How far was the failure of the White armies during the Civil War due to disunity and divided leadership?

[END OF QUESTION PAPER]

[BLANK PAGE]

X044/302

NATIONAL
QUALIFICATIONS
2006

MONDAY, 22 MAY
10.40 AM – 12.05 PM

HISTORY
HIGHER
Paper 2

Answer questions on only **one** Special Topic.

Take particular care to show clearly the Special Topic chosen. On the **front** of the answer book, **in the top right-hand corner**, write the number of the Special Topic.

You are expected to use background knowledge appropriately in answering source-based questions.

Marks may be deducted for bad spelling and bad punctuation, and for writing that is difficult to read.

Some sources have been adapted or translated.

SCOTTISH
QUALIFICATIONS
AUTHORITY

[BLANK PAGE]

OPTION A: MEDIEVAL HISTORY

SPECIAL TOPIC 1: NORMAN CONQUEST AND EXPANSION 1050–1153

Study the sources below and then answer the questions which follow.

Source A: from the Bayeux Tapestry, showing the Battle of Hastings. The wavy line under the infantry and the cavalry represents a hill.

Source B: from *The Anglo-Saxon Chronicle*.

William swore (before the Archbishop would place the crown on his head) that he would rule all his people as well as the best of the kings before him, if they would be loyal to him. All the same he taxed people very severely, and then went in spring [1067] overseas to Normandy, and took with him archbishop Stigand, and Aethelnoth, abbot of Glastonbury, and Edgar and earl Edwin and earl Morcar and earl Waltheof . . . and many other good men from England. And bishop Odo and earl William [of Hereford] stayed behind and built castles far and wide throughout this country, and distressed the wretched folk, and always after that it grew much worse. May the end be good when God wills!

Source C: from the *Ecclesiastical History* of Orderic Vitalis, written *c.* 1114–1141.

When the Norman conquest had brought such grievous burdens upon the English, Bleddyn, king of the Welsh, came to the help of his uncles, bringing a great army of Welshmen with him. After large numbers of the leading men of England and Wales had met together, a general outcry arose against the injustice and tyranny which the Normans and their comrades-in-arms had inflicted on the English.

To meet the danger the king rode to all the remote parts of his kingdom and fortified strategic sites against enemy attacks. For the fortifications called castles by the Normans were scarcely known in the English provinces, and so the English, in spite of their courage and love of fighting, could put up only a weak resistance to their enemies. The king built a castle at Warwick and gave it into the keeping of Henry, son of Roger of Beaumont. After this Edwin, Morcar and their men, unwilling to face the doubtful issue of a battle, and wisely preferring peace to war, sought the king's pardon and obtained it at least in outward appearance. Next the king built Nottingham castle and entrusted it to William Peverel.

Source D: from D. Bates, *William the Conqueror* (1989).

In the event of a Norman summoning an Englishman to defend himself on a serious criminal charge, such as perjury, murder or theft, a concession was made to English legal procedure. The Englishman was allowed to choose between ordeal by hot iron, which was used in England before 1066, or trial by combat, which was not. This admirably sums up William's attitude to the English: on the one hand, the ferocious crushing of all acts of violent resistance in the name of law and order, and on the other, the creation of mechanisms to resolve areas of social difference for those willing to live at peace.

For all the apparent efforts to achieve integration and reconciliation, the historian cannot overlook the fact that the Norman Conquest was a complete catastrophe as far as the English aristocracy was concerned. Many lost their lands and many more chose to emigrate in preference to living under Norman rule.

Source E: from H. R. Loyn, *The Norman Conquest* (1965).

William was, by reputation and in fact, one of the most active monarchs ever to have occupied the throne of England. He nevertheless remained a Norman, Duke William II of Normandy . . . William faced a very difficult political situation in the north of France . . . His main troubles came from inside his own family, especially from his eldest son Robert Curthose. Robert almost ruined the duchy, and it needed the best efforts, first of William Rufus, who held the duchy in pledge for three years when Robert was away on Crusade, and then of Henry I after his victory in 1106, to repair the damage done by their generous, irresponsible elder brother.

[END OF SOURCES FOR SPECIAL TOPIC 1]

SPECIAL TOPIC 1: NORMAN CONQUEST AND EXPANSION 1050–1153

Answer *all* of the following questions.

Marks

1. How fully does **Source A** show the tactics used by Harold and William throughout the Battle of Hastings?
Use the source and recalled knowledge.   6

2. How valuable is **Source B** as evidence of William's policy towards the English immediately after the Battle of Hastings?
In reaching a conclusion you should refer to:
   * *the origin and possible purpose of the source;*
   * *the content of the source;*
   * *recalled knowledge.*   5

3. To what extent do **Sources B** and **C** agree about the methods which William used to govern England after the conquest?
Compare the sources overall and in detail.   5

4. To what extent did William destroy Anglo-Saxon society and government?
*Use **Sources B**, **C** and **D** and recalled knowledge.*   8

5. How effectively did Henry I deal with the problems identified in **Source E**?
Use the source and recalled knowledge.   6

                                                                                                       (30)

[END OF QUESTIONS ON SPECIAL TOPIC 1]

SPECIAL TOPIC 2: THE CRUSADES 1096–1204

Study the sources below and then answer the questions which follow.

Source A: an Illumination from the thirteenth-century manuscript, "Les Histoires d'Outremer", showing the Crusaders bombarding Nicea with the severed heads of captive Muslim knights.

Source B: from an account of the Battle of Hattin, 1187 by a local Frank, "Ernoul", written soon after 1197.

King Guy and his army left the spring of Saffuriya to go to save Tiberias. As soon as they had left the water behind, Saladin ordered his skirmishers to harass them from morning until midday. The heat was so great that they could not go on to find water. The king and all the other people were spread out and did not know what to do. They could not turn back for the losses would have been too great. He sent to the count of Tripoli, who led the advance guard, to ask advice as to what to do. He sent word that he should pitch his tent and make camp. The king gladly accepted this bad advice. Some people in the army said that if the Christians had gone on to meet the Saracens, Saladin would have been defeated.

As soon as they were encamped, Saladin ordered all his men to collect brushwood, dry grass, stubble and anything else with which they could light fires, and make barriers all round the Christians. They soon did this, and the fires burned vigorously and the smoke from the fires was great. This, together with the heat of the sun, caused them discomfort and great harm. Saladin had commanded caravans of camels loaded with water from the Sea of Tiberias to be brought up and had water pots placed near the camp. The water pots were then emptied in view of the Christians so that they should have still greater anguish through thirst, and their horses too.

Source C: the Massacre of Acre, from the *Itinerarium Peregrinorum et Gesta Regis Ricardi,* a contemporary chronicle of the Third Crusade, based on eye witness accounts.

Saladin had not arranged for the return of the Holy Cross. Instead, he neglected the hostages who were held as security for its return. He hoped that by using the Holy Cross he could gain much greater concessions in negotiation. Saladin meanwhile was sending gifts and messengers to the king, gaining time by false and clever words. He fulfilled none of his promises, but attempted for a long time to keep the king from making up his mind . . .

After the time limit had more than passed, King Richard thought that Saladin had hardened his heart and cared no longer about ransoming the hostages. He assembled a council of the greater men and they decided that they would wait no longer, but that they would behead the captives. They decided, however, to set apart some of the more noble men on the chance that they might be ransomed or exchanged for some other Christian captives.

He ordered that two thousand seven hundred of the vanquished Turkish hostages be led out of the city and decapitated. Without delay his assistants rushed up and quickly carried out the order. They gave heartfelt thanks, since with the approval of divine grace they were taking vengeance in kind for the death of the Christians whom these people had slaughtered.

Source D: from T. Jones and A. Ereira, *Crusade* (1996).

Richard was anxious to get to Jerusalem and he had no intention of hanging around in Acre for the drawn-out process of ransoming prisoners. He had nearly three thousand captured Moslems on his hands. Saladin, in his situation, would have released the prisoners. In fact Saladin had already been heavily criticised by his own people for releasing so many of the prisoners of Hattin and for allowing Tyre to be reinforced with the men he had freed.

Richard agreed with these critics. He therefore took the first opportunity of a hitch in the ransom arrangements to butcher all his prisoners. Some 2700 survivors of the Moslem garrison, with three hundred of their wives and children, were taken outside the city walls in chains and slaughtered in cold blood in the sight of Saladin's army.

Source E: from D. Nicolle, *The Crusades* (2001).

Before the First Crusade, most Western European states had at best a distant relationship with the Muslims of the Eastern Mediterranean. The only exceptions were some Italian merchant republics and the Norman kingdom of Southern Italy and Sicily . . . For the merchants on both sides such links were purely commercial . . . There was surely an element of economic opportunism on the part of some Italian participants in the Crusades.

The economic impact of two centuries of Crusading warfare upon some parts of Europe was considerable. In many other areas however, this impact was negligible. While in countries such as France, Germany and England the need to raise money to finance the Crusades did play some role in the development of government financial systems, it was only in Italy that the economic impact of Crusades was really important. Even here the events of the 12th and 13th centuries were only part of the longer history of the trading relationships between the Italian states and their Islamic neighbours to the south and east.

[END OF SOURCES FOR SPECIAL TOPIC 2]

SPECIAL TOPIC 2: THE CRUSADES 1096–1204

Answer *all* of the following questions.

Marks

1. How useful is **Source A** as evidence of barbaric behaviour by the Crusaders?
   In reaching a conclusion you should refer to:
   - *the origin and possible purpose of the source;*
   - *the content of the source;*
   - *recalled knowledge.*

   5

2. How fully does **Source B** describe the events of the Battle of Hattin?
   Use the source and recalled knowledge.

   6

3. Compare the explanations for the Massacre of Acre in **Sources C** and **D**.
   Compare the sources overall and in detail.

   5

4. How fully do **Sources B**, **C** and **E** describe the crusading ideal?
   *Use **Sources B**, **C** and **E** and recalled knowledge.*

   8

5. To what extent do you agree with David Nicolle's view in **Source E** about the economic impact of the Crusades throughout Europe.
   Use the source and recalled knowledge.

   6

   (30)

[END OF QUESTIONS ON SPECIAL TOPIC 2]

OPTION B: EARLY MODERN HISTORY

SPECIAL TOPIC 3: SCOTLAND 1689–1715

Study the sources below and then answer the questions which follow.

Source A: from P. W. J. Riley, *The Union of Scotland and England* (1978).

From the parliament of 1703 emerged the Act Anent Peace and War and the Act of Security, both forced on the court by the ill-assorted opposition and both important links in the chain of events leading to the union. The first Act invested in the Scottish parliament for the future, the final decision on Scotland's declaring war. The prospect worried Godolphin but, despite his private protests to the Scottish officers of state, the queen was advised to let it become law. The Act of Security was intended to lay down the conditions under which the next successor to the Scottish throne was to be selected, conditions which would ensure that the choice was free of English influence. For the English the alarming part of the Act was the "communication of trade" clause. By this provision the separation of England and Scotland was envisaged on the death of the queen unless, in the meantime, the Scots had been granted amongst other things, full freedom of trade with England and her colonies.

Source B: from James Hodges, *The Rights and Interests of the Two British Monarchies* (1703).

There is a proposal for a federal union under one Monarch. In it, there shall be no other alteration in the constitutions of either Kingdom, but that each . . . are to retain their National Distinction, to enjoy their particular Liberties, Privileges, and Independence, and to hold their different governments in Church and State, with the laws, customs and rights of the same, as they did before the Union . . . This kind of union is different from that, which some insist upon for uniting the two into one kingdom, one government, one parliament etc under the title of an incorporating union . . .

A federal union is much more agreeable to the real interests of both nations . . . But it is simply impossible to consult the true interests of either nation by an incorporating union, however contrived or qualified.

Source C: from a speech by Seton of Pitmedden in the Scots Parliament, 1706.

There can be no sure guarantee for the observance of the articles of a federal union between two nations, where one is much superior to the other in riches, numbers of people and an extended commerce. Do the advantages of a federal union balance its disadvantages? Will the English accept a federal union, supposing it to be for the true interest of both nations? No federal union between Scotland and England is sufficient to secure the peace of this island, or fortify it against the intrigues and invasions of its foreign enemies. England should not give its trade and protection to this nation till both kingdoms are incorporated into one.

Source D: from Houston and Knox (eds), *The New Penguin History of Scotland* (2001).

The first vote on Article one of the Act, requiring that "the two Kingdoms of England and Scotland shall . . . be united into one Kingdom by the name of Great Britain", resulted in a crown majority of thirty-three, a comfortable but not an entirely reassuring result. The government was especially concerned about the influence of the Church of Scotland, and therefore passed a separate Act guaranteeing its Presbyterian future. This removed a good deal of popular resistance, as well as calming opposition among the Whig-Presbyterian interest in the chamber. Promises to pay off Darien investors from the Equivalent, a large lump sum of £398,085 10s sterling, persuaded Tweeddale's New Party to unite with the court. There is no question that Queensberry used the usual methods of bribery and coercion, including £20,000 sterling from the English treasury, to stiffen the resolve of government supporters who were awaiting arrears of their salaries.

Source E: from a letter written by the earl of Mar to the earl of Leven, 1708.

The Queen called a Cabinet Council last night, where she was pleased to call the dukes of Queensberry and Montrose, the earl of Loudon, Seafield and myself. We gave an account there of what orders the Queen had sent to Scotland, since the news of the invasion . . . It is expected that the Council will seize the horses and arms of those they think disloyal, and will also be giving their advice and instructions for securing the money, in the Mint and Bank, in case of a [hostile] landing . . . It was told to us that since both Houses had advised the Queen to arrest such persons as she had cause to suspect, and are now discussing a Bill for the suspending of Habeas Corpus Acts, it was appropriate that suspected people in Scotland should be arrested.

[*END OF SOURCES FOR SPECIAL TOPIC 3*]

SPECIAL TOPIC 3: SCOTLAND 1689–1715

Answer *all* of the following questions.

Marks

1. How far does **Source A** explain why relations between Scotland and England were strained in the period 1689 – 1705?
   Use the source and recalled knowledge.   **7**

2. Compare the attitudes towards Union expressed in **Sources B** and **C**.
   Compare the sources overall and in detail.   **5**

3. How typical is **Source C** of the opinions of Scottish supporters of Union?
   Use the source and recalled knowledge.   **5**

4. How fully do **Sources A**, **C**, and **D** explain the reasons for the passing of the Treaty of Union?
   *Use **Sources A**, **C** and **D** and recalled knowledge.*   **8**

5. How valuable is **Source E** as evidence of immediate problems following the Union?
   In reaching a conclusion you should refer to:
   • *the origin and possible purpose of the source;*
   • *the content of the source;*
   • *recalled knowledge.*   **5**

                                                                                                    (30)

[*END OF QUESTIONS ON SPECIAL TOPIC 3*]

SPECIAL TOPIC 4: THE ATLANTIC SLAVE TRADE

Study the sources below and then answer the questions which follow.

Source A: from Stephen Fuller, *Remarks on the Resolution of the West India Planters and Merchants* (1789).

In certain vast regions of the African continent, where the arts of rural cultivation are little known, the number of inhabitants grows faster than the means of sustaining them. Humane concerns force the sending of the surplus, as objects of traffic, to more enlightened, or less populous countries. These countries, standing in constant need of their labour, receive them into property, protection and employment.

Source B: from Peter J. Kitson, *Slavery, Abolition and Emancipation: Volume 2—The Abolition Debate* (1999).

The anti-slavery movement was made up of several different perspectives: philosophical, religious, economic, legal and political . . . In Britain many of the leading thinkers were opposed to slavery . . . Adam Smith insisted that freemen would work better than slaves and that slave labour is the most expensive form of labour . . . By the close of the eighteenth century, the slave trade was largely regarded as contrary to religion, nature and justice . . . The contribution of the Friends [Quakers] to anti-slavery opinion was vital. They believed that slavery was against the will of God as revealed in the Old and New Testaments.

Another important factor in the growth of the opposition against the slave trade was the rise in evangelical Christianity in Great Britain in the late eighteenth century, members of which increasingly came to regard slavery as contrary to the law of Christian love. The evangelical Christians combined a belief in a universal humanity with a strong sense of individual guilt as well as a desire to relieve the sufferings of people through good works.

Source C: from a petition to Parliament, from the Archdeaconry of Leicester, quoted in *Gentleman's Magazine LXII* (1792).

As Ministers of that Holy Religion which promotes universal love, we feel bound humbly to protest against a traffic, which is a constant violation of the most essential duties of Christianity. This, if continued under the sanction of the British Legislature, may be expected to bring down upon this country the severest judgement of Heaven.

Source D: from a speech in the House of Commons by Bamber Gasgoyne, 1806.

The attempts to make a popular outcry against this trade were never so conspicuous as in the late election, when the public newspapers teemed with abuse . . . and when promises were required from the different candidates that they would oppose its continuance There never had been any question since that of parliamentary reform in which so much energy had been exerted to raise a popular prejudice . . . in every manufacturing town and borough.

Every measure that invention or skill could devise to create a popular outcry was resorted to on this occasion. The Church, the theatre and the press had laboured to create a prejudice against the Slave Trade.

Source E: from Adrian Hastings, "Abolitionists Black and White", in D. Northrup (ed), *The Atlantic Slave Trade* (2002).

In 1807, the bill for the abolition of the slave trade was passed by the British Parliament, just twenty years after the Abolition Committee was first formed in London. It was, despite the delay (in large part due to the counter-effect of the French Revolution and the war), an impressive achievement.

It was managed by the combination of an efficient "moderate" leadership, at once religious and political, with a nation-wide public opinion produced by a great deal of campaigning. The sustained parliamentary spokesmanship of Wilberforce, personal friend for so many years of the Prime Minister, was invaluable, though the true architects of abolition were Granville Sharp and Thomas Clarkson. A cause which in the early 1780s still seemed eccentric was rendered respectable by the underlying support of the two greatest parliamentarians of the age – Pitt and Fox. It would certainly not have been carried through without very powerful religious convictions at work. It seems hard to deny that it was due to the persevering commitment to the abolitionist cause of quite a small group of men whose separate abilities and positions were knitted together to form a lobby of exceptional effectiveness.

[END OF SOURCES FOR SPECIAL TOPIC 4]

SPECIAL TOPIC 4: THE ATLANTIC SLAVE TRADE

Answer *all* of the following questions.   *Marks*

1. How typical is the evidence in **Source A** of the arguments used by supporters of the Slave Trade?
    Use the source and recalled knowledge.   **6**

2. To what extent does the evidence in **Source C** support **Source B**'s assessment of the reasons for opposition to the Slave Trade?
    Compare the sources overall and in detail.   **4**

3. How useful is **Source D** as evidence of the methods used by the abolitionists to promote their cause?
    In reaching a conclusion you should refer to:
    *   *the origin and possible purpose of the source;*
    *   *the content of the source;*
    *   *recalled knowledge.*   **5**

4. How fully do **Sources A**, **B** and **E** identify the issues in the debate over the Slave Trade?
    *Use **Sources A, B** and **E** and recalled knowledge.*   **8**

5. How adequate is the explanation given in **Source E** for the eventual abolition of the Slave Trade in 1807?
    Use the source and recalled knowledge.   **7**

                                                                                                                    (30)

[END OF QUESTIONS ON SPECIAL TOPIC 4]

SPECIAL TOPIC 5: THE AMERICAN REVOLUTION

Study the sources below and then answer the questions which follow.

Source A: from an article by Dr Samuel Johnson, 1774.

No man is a patriot who justifies the ridiculous claims of the Americans, or who tries to deprive the British nation of its natural and lawful authority over its own colonies (those colonies, which were settled under British protection, were constituted by a British charter and have been defended by British arms).

It is absurd to suppose, that by founding a colony, the nation established an independent power. It is equally absurd to think that when emigrants become rich they shall not contribute to their own defence unless they choose to do so and that they shall not be included in the general system of representation.

He that accepts protection, promises obedience. We have always protected the Americans. We may, therefore, subject them to government. . . . The parliament may enact, for America, a law of capital punishment. It may, therefore, establish a method and level of taxation.

Source B: from a letter from Lord Barrington, Secretary at War, to Dartmouth, American Secretary, 24 December 1774.

I do not believe any ministry will ever attempt another internal tax on the North Americans by Act of Parliament. Experience has shown we do not have the strength in that part of the world to levy such taxes, against a universal opinion prevailing there that we have no right to levy them. Many among ourselves, though persuaded of the right, doubt at least the fairness of such taxations; as the Parliament knows little about the state of the colonies and as the members of neither House are to pay any part of the burden they impose.

Source C: from D. Higginbotham, "The War for Independence, to Saratoga", in J. Greene and J.R. Pole (eds), *A Companion to the American Revolution* (2000).

The campaign of 1776 saw Britain take the offensive; but it is hardly accurate to say that she possessed the lion's share of the advantages. Problems of transportation, communication and supply were serious concerns two hundred years ago. So were her lack of sufficient men under arms. Her generals and admirals were competent enough, though little more than that—Generals Gage, Howe and Clinton were too cautious; Burgoyne and Cornwallis were too aggressive. Admiral Howe was hesitant. Clinton called Howe's naval successors "old women" who got along poorly with their army counterparts. The British generals in America, who were Members of Parliament with alliances to rival political factions, also distrusted each other.

Source D: from a British Officer, describing the retreat of Washington's forces from New York, 1776.

As we go forward into the country, the rebels flee before us, and when we come back they always follow us. It's almost impossible to catch them. They will neither fight, nor totally run away, but they keep at such distance that we are always above a day's march from them. They seem to be playing at hide and seek.

Source E: from a letter from Lord Cornwallis to General Clinton, written at Yorktown, October 20, 1781.

Sir, I am ashamed to inform your Excellency that I have been forced to give up the posts of York and Gloucester and to surrender the troops under my command by surrendering on the 19th of this month as prisoners of war to the combined forces of America and France.

I never saw this command at Yorktown in a very favourable light . . . Only the hope of reinforcement or rescue made me attempt its defence. Otherwise I would either have tried to escape to New York by rapid marches from the Gloucester side immediately on the arrival of General Washington's troops at Williamsburgh, or I would, despite the inequality of numbers, have attacked them in the open field . . . But being assured by your Excellency's letters that every possible means would be tried by the navy and army to relieve us, I could not think myself able to attempt either of those desperate measures . . .

[END OF SOURCES FOR SPECIAL TOPIC 5]

SPECIAL TOPIC 5: THE AMERICAN REVOLUTION

Answer *all* of the following questions.

Marks

1. How accurately does **Source A** identify the issues that led to the colonial challenge to British control in America?
   Use the source and recalled knowledge.

   7

2. Compare the views expressed in **Sources A** and **B** on the question of taxing America.
   Compare the sources overall and in detail.

   5

3. How adequately does **Source C** explain the problems faced by Britain after the outbreak of war in America?
   Use the source and recalled knowledge.

   6

4. How useful is **Source D** as evidence of the tactics used by colonial troops in the war?
   In reaching a conclusion you should refer to:
   * *the origin and possible purpose of the source;*
   * *the content of the source;*
   * *recalled knowledge.*

   4

5. How fully do **Sources C, D** and **E** explain the reasons for colonial victory in the war?
   *Use **Sources C, D** and **E** and recalled knowledge.*

   8

   (30)

[END OF QUESTIONS ON SPECIAL TOPIC 5]

OPTION C: LATER MODERN HISTORY

SPECIAL TOPIC 6: PATTERNS OF MIGRATION: SCOTLAND 1830s–1930s

Study the sources below and then answer the questions which follow.

Source A: from *Glasgow Past and Present*, 23 July 1849.

There are not less than 50,000 Irish people, or of Irish descent, in Glasgow. A very small proportion of these, as compared with Catholics, are Orangemen or Protestants. In 1846, according to information kindly supplied by the Bishop, no fewer than 3,000 children were baptised in the various Catholic places of worship in the city.

A gentleman, still living, remembers when the first Irishman planted himself down in Gorbals, where he was considered as much a curiosity for a time as if he had been a tattooed New Zealander. At the present moment the principal parts of Gorbals, in Main Street and its vicinity, are almost entirely in the possession of these invaders who, however, are generally an orderly and hard working class of people. They give little trouble to the police, as compared with their countrymen in other parts of the city. Further, Mr. R. Lindsay remembers when the first Irishman wriggled himself into the locality of Fiddlers' Close and the man was tolerated by the Scotch inhabitants by reason of his agreeing to keep the close clean.

Source B: from R. Swift and S. Gilley (eds), *The Irish in the Victorian City* (1985).

The Irish were thoroughly disliked and feared for the problems which they brought in their wake. Not the least of these was disease. Typhus was sometimes called "famine disease" or "Irish fever", and its association with the Irish hastened the emergence of distinct ghettoes or "Little Irelands". Some of the Irish rejected the housing standards of the native poor and were condemned for their unhygienic habits. The expectations of most immigrants were set by what was commonplace in Ireland, but Ireland was much poorer than Britain. The prominence of the Irish in the crime statistics was another cause of complaint, although their offences were mostly of a minor nature—drunkenness, petty theft and offences against the person. There were numerous complaints about the Irish share of poor relief in areas of heavy immigration . . . Indeed, many viewed the arrival of the Irish as a social disaster and residential segregation set them apart from the local population.

Source C: from the *Aberdeen Herald*, 4 December 1852.

The farm workers were honest, plain, hard-working men, who looked forward to the day when they or their sons would be able to get larger and larger farms as their honest savings increased. These men, in many cases, have been obliged, along with their families, to leave for our towns in order to get employment, or have emigrated to countries where their skill and hard work will be more highly appreciated. A farm servant, who may have saved fifty or sixty pounds, can not even get a small farm upon which he might invest his small sum of money. His only refuge is a foreign land; and thus it is that our very best agricultural labourers are driven from this country by the foolishness of "penny wise and pound foolish" landowners . . . It is clear that the cold and damp bothy will not persuade our young ploughmen to remain at home and give up their chance of comfort, if not wealth, in America or Australia.

Source D: from a statement by George Wood, a Scottish emigrant to Canada, 1842.

I emigrated to this country with my wife and five children seven years ago. We all have enjoyed good health as the climate in this part of the country is remarkably healthy. I consider that the change by emigrating here is to my advantage, and that of my family. I am quite in a different situation now in this country as regards acquired property from what I would have been in had I remained in Scotland. By adopting this country as the future home of myself and family, I am now a master, where I could never well expect otherwise than to see myself and my family as servants in the old country. The ease of acquiring property here is great, and any man, single or married, of sober, economical, hardworking and persevering habits is sure to do well.

Source E: from "Scotland's Story", a Scottish Television Production (1988).

The religious divide lasted well into the twentieth century. It was hard for a Catholic to make progress up the social and career ladder in certain jobs. Few Catholics obtained employment in the shipyards; the medical profession (not openly) did not encourage doctors from certain schools to enter some areas of medicine. Irish Catholics thus found things more difficult. It is fair to say however, that working class people of all faiths found progress in certain professions more difficult than middle class people.

[END OF SOURCES FOR SPECIAL TOPIC 6]

SPECIAL TOPIC 6: PATTERNS OF MIGRATION: SCOTLAND 1830s–1930s

Answer *all* of the following questions.   *Marks*

1. To what extent does **Source A** reflect Scottish attitudes towards Irish immigrants in the mid-nineteenth century?
    Use the source and recalled knowledge.   **6**

2. How far does the evidence in **Source A** support the views of the historian in **Source B** about the impact of Irish immigration on life in Scotland?
    Compare the sources overall and in detail.   **5**

3. How useful is **Source C** as evidence of the reasons for Scottish emigration during the period from the 1830s to the 1930s?
    In reaching a conclusion you should refer to:
    *   *the origin and possible purpose of the source;*
    *   *the content of the source;*
    *   *recalled knowledge.*   **5**

4. How typical were the experiences of George Wood (**Source D**) of Scottish emigrants between the 1830s and 1930s?
    Use the source and recalled knowledge.   **6**

5. How successful were immigrant groups in being accepted as part of Scottish society between the 1830s and 1930s?
    *Use **Sources A**, **B** and **E** and recalled knowledge.*   **8**

    (30)

[END OF QUESTIONS ON SPECIAL TOPIC 6]

SPECIAL TOPIC 7: APPEASEMENT AND THE ROAD TO WAR, TO 1939

Study the sources below and then answer the questions which follow.

Source A: from a letter written by a young American member of the International Brigade, 1938.

Somewhere in Spain

In the event of my death, will the finder please mail this letter to my mother?

Dear Mom

In Spain there are countless thousands of mothers like yourself who never had a fair chance in life. One day the Spanish people did something about that. They got together and elected a government that really gave some meaning to their lives. But it didn't work out the way the poor people expected. A group of bullies decided to crush and wipe out this wonderful thing the poor people had accomplished and drive them back to the old way of life.

Don't let anyone mislead you, Mom, by telling you that all this had something to do with Communism. The Hitlers and Mussolinis of this world are killing Spanish people who don't know the difference between Communism and rheumatism. And it's not to set up some Communist government, either. The only thing the Communists did here was to show the people how to fight and win what is rightfully theirs.

I was always proud and grateful that you were my Mom.

Your son

Will

Source B: from a speech by Winston Churchill in the House of Commons, 19 July 1937.

It is well known that ordinary guarantees for safety and order had largely lapsed in Spain, that it was not safe for people to go out at night over large areas, that murders and outrages were rife. Constitutional parliamentary government was being used . . . to cover the swift, stealthy and deadly advance of the extreme Communist or anarchist factions. They saw, according to the regular programme of Communist revolutions, the means by which they could obtain power. It was when confronted with a situation like that, that this violent explosion [the Civil War] took place in Spain.

Source C: from Andrew Boxer, *Appeasement* (1998).

The record of British foreign policy in this period [1930–1937] looks grim. The failure to resist aggression in Abyssinia encouraged the dictators and destroyed the credibility of the League of Nations. Italy was alienated as a potential ally. Aggression in Spain was ignored. Britain accepted Hitler's destruction of the military clauses of the Treaty of Versailles without gaining much in return. Significant differences developed between Britain and France about how to handle the dictators.

Source D: from a speech by Viscount Astor in Parliament, 16 March 1938.

By our failure to settle certain questions in the past we must bear a certain measure of responsibility for the way in which things have happened. By the peace treaties the Austrian-Hungarian Empire was broken up and its population divided. As a result we had economic distress in Austria. The Schuschnigg government was felt to be a weak government and there was a tendency for people to drift either to Nazis or Communists.

At present I do not believe that any government, whether democratic or totalitarian, can face the possibility of a world war. Now the long range bomber means the civilian population of Germany will suffer as much as the civilian population elsewhere. It is likely that another war will be followed by revolution and the growth of Communism. Therefore I do not think any country will consider war. I cannot help thinking the way is still open to negotiation which will lead to some all round settlement. At all events it is worth exploring. There are only two alternatives I can see. One is to talk; the other is a blind drift to war.

Source E: the cover of the Italian magazine, *Illustrazione del Popolo*, 9-15 October 1938.

1° OTTOBRE 1938: UNA DATA STORICA.
Le truppe liberatrici entrano nelle terre sudetiche restituite alla Germania
in virtù del Protocollo di Monaco.

The caption reads, " 1st October 1938: a historic date. The liberating troops enter the Sudetenland restored to Germany through the Munich agreement".

[*END OF SOURCES FOR SPECIAL TOPIC 7*]

SPECIAL TOPIC 7: APPEASEMENT AND THE ROAD TO WAR, TO 1939

Answer *all* of the following questions.   *Marks*

1. How valuable is **Source A** as evidence of the motives of members of the International Brigade during the Spanish Civil War?
    In reaching a conclusion you should refer to:
    *   *the origin and possible purpose of the source;*
    *   *the content of the source;*
    *   *recalled knowledge.*   5

2. Compare the views about the Spanish Civil War expressed in **Sources A** and **B**.
    Compare the sources overall and in detail.   5

3. How far to do you agree with **Source C**'s assessment of British foreign policy up to 1937?
    Use the source and recalled knowledge.   6

4. How typical is **Source E** of international reactions to the Munich agreement?
    Use the source and recalled knowledge.   6

5. How fully do **Sources A**, **D** and **E** illustrate attitudes towards appeasement during the late 1930s?
    *Use Sources **A**, **D** and **E** and recalled knowledge.*   8

[*END OF QUESTIONS ON SPECIAL TOPIC 7*]   **(30)**

SPECIAL TOPIC 8: THE ORIGINS AND DEVELOPMENT OF THE COLD WAR 1945–1985

Study the sources below and then answer the questions which follow.

Source A: from a report by Simon Bourgin, an American journalist in Budapest, 5 July 1956.

The events that started in Moscow with the de-Stalinisation program have more than ever begun to have some kind of influence in Hungary—things are now moving at a pace where the results cannot be predicted . . .

On 27th June, I attended a meeting of the Petofi Club, for writers and authors. There were about 2000 people in the audience, about a third of them army officers . . .

One of the speakers was a young lady from the University of Budapest. In her speech she stated that the people in the regime had lost touch with the rank and file of the Party, and with the common people altogether. They bought their clothes and food out of special shops in Budapest, they lived in expensive five-room villas. They had forgotten that most people were crowded one family to a room, and that a lot of people in Budapest did not have enough to eat. She finished by saying that there absolutely had to be a change in Party leadership.

Source B: from W.R. Keylor, *The Twentieth Century World* (4th edn., 2001).

The prospect of a politically independent and militarily neutral Hungary was evidently too much for the Soviet leadership to accept. It would establish a dangerous precedent that, if followed by the other East European states, could only bring about the disintegration of the buffer zone between Russia and the West, which Russia had established after the collapse of Hitler's Reich. The "liberation" of the Soviet East European Empire and the "rollback" of Communist power to the Russian frontier suddenly seemed imminent, not because of American pressure, but because of the explosion of unrestrained nationalism in Hungary.

On 4 November 1956, the Russian Army returned in force to Budapest. The Nagy government was forcibly replaced by a puppet government under Janos Kadar, whose authority rested entirely on the presence of Soviet troops.

Source C: from A. Dobson and S. Marsh, *US Foreign Policy since 1945* (2001).

After the Americans discovered the Russian missiles in Cuba, there was never any argument about the fact that they had to go. They could not stay for three basic reasons . . .

First, they would have had a psychological impact which would have been very damaging politically . . . It was bad enough having a communist state in the Western hemisphere—one with nuclear weapons was just not acceptable. It would have altered the perceptions of the relative standing of the USA and the Soviet Union in the Cold War and, as Kennedy commented, perceptions contribute to reality.

Second, the missiles would have strengthened the Soviet Union's strike capability and cut down the warning time.

Third, it might have encouraged the Russians to take other chances, risking unintentional nuclear war.

Source D: from a policy Memorandum by Dean Rusk (Secretary of State) and Robert McNamara (Secretary of Defence) to President Kennedy, 1961.

The deteriorating situation in South Vietnam requires the attention of the United States. The loss of South Vietnam to communism would involve the transfer of a nation of 20 million people from the free world to the Communist bloc . . . We would have to face the near certainty that the rest of Southeast Asia would move closer to communism . . .

The United States should commit itself to the clear objective of preventing the fall of South Vietnam to communism . . . We must try to put the government of South Vietnam into a position to win its own war against the communist guerrillas. We should also be prepared to introduce United States combat forces if that should become necessary for success . . . It may also be necessary for United States forces to strike at the source of the aggression in North Vietnam.

Source E: from a speech by Senator Mike Mansfield, 1962.

If our present level of support for South Vietnam does not work, it is difficult to conceive of alternatives, with the possible exception of a truly massive commitment of American military personnel—in short, going to war ourselves against the guerrillas.

That is an alternative which I most emphatically do not recommend. On the contrary, it seems to me most essential that we make it crystal clear to South Vietnam that, while we will go to great lengths to help, the primary responsibility rests with the Vietnamese. It is their country, their future which is most at stake, not ours. To ignore that reality will not only be immensely costly in terms of American lives and resources, but it may also draw us into a conflict which we cannot win.

[END OF SOURCES FOR SPECIAL TOPIC 8]

SPECIAL TOPIC 8: THE ORIGINS AND DEVELOPMENT OF THE COLD WAR 1945–1985

Answer *all* of the following questions.

Marks

1. How valuable is **Source A** as evidence of the growth of discontent in Hungary in 1956?
In reaching a conclusion you should refer to:
   * *the origin and possible purpose of the source;*
   * *the content of the source;*
   * *recalled knowledge.*   **5**

2. How fully does **Source B** explain the reasons for the actions taken by the USSR in Hungary in 1956?
Use the source and recalled knowledge.   **6**

3. To what extent do the views expressed in **Source C** explain American concerns and actions over Cuba in 1962?
Use the source and recalled knowledge.   **6**

4. Compare the views in **Sources D** and **E** on the case for American military involvement in Vietnam.
Compare the sources overall and in detail.   **5**

5. How adequately do **Sources B**, **C** and **D** explain the reasons for tension between the Superpowers up to the mid-1960s?
*Use **Sources B**, **C** and **D** and recalled knowledge.*   **8**

(30)

[END OF QUESTIONS ON SPECIAL TOPIC 8]

SPECIAL TOPIC 9: IRELAND 1900–1985: A DIVIDED IDENTITY

Study the sources below and then answer the questions which follow.

Source A: from a speech by John Redmond in the House of Commons, 15 September 1914.

For the first time . . . Ireland in this war feels her interests are precisely the same as yours. She feels that British democracy has kept faith with her . . . The men of Ireland will spring to your aid in this war.

I have promised publicly, on hundreds of platforms during the last few years, that when the rights of Ireland were accepted by the democracy of England, then Ireland would become the strongest arm in the defence of the Empire.

I would feel personally dishonoured if I did not say to my fellow-countrymen that it is their duty, and should be their honour, to take their place in the firing line in this contest.

Source B: from an article by Arthur Griffith in *Sinn Féin* newspaper, 8 August 1914.

Ireland is not at war with Germany. She has no quarrel with any Continental power. England is at war with Germany, and Mr. Redmond has offered England the services of the Irish Volunteers to "defend Ireland". What has Ireland to defend, and whom has she to defend it against?

There is no European power waging war against the people of Ireland. There are two European powers at war with the people who dominate Ireland from Dublin Castle.

Our duty is not in doubt. We are Irish Nationalists and the only duty we can have is to stand for Ireland's interests, irrespective of the interests of England or Germany or any other foreign country.

Source C: from an article in the *Irish Times*, 1 May 1916.

It is believed that most of the leaders of the Rising are dead or captured. So ends the criminal adventure of the men who declared that they were "striking in full confidence of victory" and that they would be supported by "gallant allies in Europe".

The gallant allies' only gift to them was an Irish renegade [Roger Casement]. Ireland has been saved from shame and ruin, and the whole Empire from a serious danger. Where our politicians failed, the British army has won the day.

Treason must be rooted out of Ireland once and for all. The violence and bloodshed of the past week must be finished with a severity which will make any repetition of them impossible for generations to come.

Source D: from F.S.L. Lyons, "The Rising and After", in W.E. Vaughan (ed.), *A New History of Ireland* (1996).

The initial unpopularity of the Rising should have been regarded by the British government as a priceless asset. This indeed it would have been, if it had not been squandered in part, by the policy of internment. This herded innocent men and women into camps alongside dedicated revolutionaries, and exposed them to a process of indoctrination of which the full consequences were only to be seen in the years that lay ahead.

In addition, the asset of public hostility to the Rising was squandered by the policy adopted towards its leaders. Not only were they tried by secret courts martial, but the executions were spun out over ten days. This was sufficient time for feelings of compassion for the victims and anger against the authorities to replace the original public condemnation of the Rising.

Source E: from J. Smith, *Britain and Ireland: From Home Rule to Independence* (2000).

The Anglo-Irish War was little more than a dirty war between hard men and gangsters on both sides—men who were incapable of adjusting to the normalities of peace, after the bloodletting of the Great War. It was a conflict characterised by spies and informers, of midnight executions, and a bullet in the back of the head—of guilt by association or family or religion, and of widespread intimidation of ordinary people by both sides.

Yet, it was a war neither side could win. As the reality of this sunk in by the summer of 1921, the British moved haltingly towards truce, which was formally agreed on 11 July, and opened the way to more formal peace negotiations.

[END OF SOURCES FOR SPECIAL TOPIC 9]

SPECIAL TOPIC 9: IRELAND 1900–1985: A DIVIDED IDENTITY

Answer *all* of the following questions.

Marks

1. How reliable is **Source A** as evidence of Irish attitudes towards supporting Britain in the First World War?
   In reaching a conclusion you should refer to:
   * *the origin and possible purpose of the source;*
   * *the content of the source;*
   * *recalled knowledge.*   5

2. Compare the attitudes in **Sources A** and **B** on Irish support for Britain in the First World War.
   Compare the sources overall and in detail.   5

3. How fully does **Source C** illustrate Irish reactions to the Easter Rising?
   Use the source and recalled knowledge.   6

4. To what extent does **Source D** explain the effects of the Easter Rising on Ireland up to 1921?
   Use the source and recalled knowledge.   6

5. Why was it so difficult to achieve a peaceful settlement in Ireland in the period after 1914?
   *Use **Sources B**, **D** and **E** and recalled knowledge.*   8

                                                                              (30)

[END OF QUESTIONS ON SPECIAL TOPIC 9]

[END OF QUESTION PAPER]

[BLANK PAGE]

[BLANK PAGE]

X044/301

NATIONAL
QUALIFICATIONS
2007

FRIDAY, 18 MAY
9.00 AM – 10.20 AM

HISTORY
HIGHER
Paper 1

Answer questions on **one** Option only.

Take particular care to show clearly the Option chosen. On the **front** of the answer book, **in the top right-hand corner**, write A or B or C.

Within the Option chosen, answer **two** questions, one from Historical Study: Scottish and British and one from Historical Study: European and World.

All questions are assigned 25 marks.

Marks may be deducted for bad spelling and bad punctuation, and for writing that is difficult to read.

SCOTTISH
QUALIFICATIONS
AUTHORITY

[BLANK PAGE]

OPTION A: MEDIEVAL HISTORY

**Answer TWO questions, one from Historical Study: Scottish and British
and one from Historical Study: European and World**

Historical Study: Scottish and British

Medieval Society

1. "Kings and barons received all of the benefits from the feudal system while peasants received none." Discuss.

2. To what extent was the medieval Church the most significant influence in people's everyday lives?

3. How important was the desire for protection in the development of towns in England and Scotland?

4. "David I was responsible for transforming Scotland from a Celtic to a feudal kingdom." How accurate is this statement?

5. How successfully did Henry II overcome the challenges that faced the monarchy when he became king?

Historical Study: European and World

EITHER

Nation and King

6. To what extent was the Magna Carta a consequence of John's failure to retain Normandy?

7. "The growth in the power of the Capetian monarchy was entirely due to the abilities and leadership of Philip II." Discuss.

8. Was the victory at Stirling Bridge William Wallace's only important contribution to the Scottish struggle for independence?

9. How far was the Scottish victory in the Wars of Independence due to their own efforts rather than English failings?

OR

Crisis of Authority

10. To what extent was the Peasants' Revolt due to the Black Death?

11. What was the main cause of the Hundred Years' War?

12. How far was Scottish involvement the main cause of the English defeat in the Hundred Years' War?

13. "The move to Avignon was the most important reason for the decline of the power of the Papacy in the fourteenth and fifteenth centuries." Discuss.

OPTION B: EARLY MODERN HISTORY

Answer TWO questions, one from Historical Study: Scottish and British and one from Historical Study: European and World

Historical Study: Scottish and British

EITHER

Scotland in the Age of the Reformation 1542–1603

1. How great an influence did the "rough wooing", 1543–1548, have on Scottish politics?

2. To what extent did the Reformation of 1560 come about for political reasons?

3. How successful were the Regents in ruling Scotland between 1567 and 1580?

4. Was Andrew Melville the main cause of religious conflict during the reign of James VI up to 1603?

5. To what extent was the power of the Scottish Crown damaged between 1542 and 1603?

OR

Scotland and England in the Century of Revolutions 1603–1702

6. How effective was James VI and I's rule in Scotland after the Union of Crowns, 1603?

7. "Eleven years of tyranny." How justified is this description of the personal rule of Charles I from 1629 to 1640?

8. "Parliament's actions between 1640 and 1642 were the most important cause of the outbreak of Civil War." How accurate is this statement?

9. How significant an impact did the Glorious Revolution of 1689 have on the government of Scotland and England?

10. To what extent did Parliament win in its struggles with the kings in the seventeenth century?

Historical Study: European and World

EITHER

Royal Authority in 17th and 18th Century Europe

11. How important was Versailles to the power of the absolute monarchy of Louis XIV?

12. Did Louis XIV revoke the Edict of Nantes in 1685 for purely religious reasons?

13. How beneficial were Frederick II's social reforms in Prussia?

14. How successfully did Joseph II deal with religious issues in Austria?

OR

The French Revolution: The Emergence of the Citizen State

15. Which section of French society had the most cause for complaint under the Ancien Régime?

16. Why did the challenge to absolute monarchy develop into revolution in 1789?

17. To what extent was Robespierre responsible for the "Terror"?

18. How important was war in causing political instability in France in the 1790s?

[Turn over

OPTION C: LATER MODERN HISTORY

**Answer TWO questions, one from Historical Study: Scottish and British
and one from Historical Study: European and World**

Historical Study: Scottish and British

Britain 1850s–1979

1. "It was the militant suffragette campaign, more than any other factor, that led to the achievement of female suffrage in 1918." How valid is this view?

2. How democratic had Britain become by 1928?

3. To what extent were the Liberal social reforms of 1906–1914 a response to the challenge from the Labour Party?

4. How successfully did the Labour government of 1945–1951 deal with the social problems identified in the Beveridge Report of 1942?

5. **Either**

    (*a*) Assess the impact of urbanisation on religion, education and leisure habits in Scotland between 1880 and 1939.

    Or

    (*b*) How far did attitudes in Scotland towards the Union change between 1880 and 1939?

Historical Study: European and World

EITHER

The Growth of Nationalism

6. To what extent was there a growth in nationalism in **either** Germany **or** Italy between 1815 and 1848?

7. **Either**

   (*a*) How important was Prussian economic growth in bringing about the unification of Germany by 1871?

   Or

   (*b*) "Foreign intervention was the main reason for the achievement of Italian unification by 1871." How justified is this view?

8. **Either**

   (*a*) How important was the leadership of Hitler in the rise of the Nazis to power in Germany by 1933?

   Or

   (*b*) How important was the leadership of Mussolini in the rise of the Fascists to power in Italy by 1922?

9. To what extent did Fascist governments rely on force to stay in power?

   Discuss with reference to **either** Nazi rule in Germany between 1933 and 1939 **or** Fascist rule in Italy between 1922 and 1939.

OR

The Large Scale State

The USA

10. To what extent were the difficulties faced by black Americans in the 1920s and 1930s due to the lack of action by the federal government?

11. "The Wall Street Crash was the principal reason for the depression of the 1930s." How justified is this view?

12. How important in restoring prosperity in the 1930s were the increased powers of the federal government under the New Deal?

13. "The Civil Rights campaign of the 1950s and 1960s concerned itself above all with the problems facing black Americans in the Southern states." How accurate is this statement?

Russia

14. "The power of the Church was the key factor in the stability of the Tsarist state in the years before 1905." How justified is this view?

15. How important was the work of Stolypin in the recovery of the Tsarist state after 1905?

16. To what extent was the Provisional Government responsible for its own downfall?

17. How effectively had the Bolsheviks established their authority over Russia by 1921?

[END OF QUESTION PAPER]

[BLANK PAGE]

X044/302

NATIONAL
QUALIFICATIONS
2007

FRIDAY, 18 MAY
10.40 AM – 12.05 PM

HISTORY
HIGHER
Paper 2

Answer questions on only **one** Special Topic.

Take particular care to show clearly the Special Topic chosen. On the **front** of the answer book, **in the top right-hand corner**, write the number of the Special Topic.

You are expected to use background knowledge appropriately in answering source-based questions.

Marks may be deducted for bad spelling and bad punctuation, and for writing that is difficult to read.

Some sources have been adapted or translated.

SCOTTISH
QUALIFICATIONS
AUTHORITY

[BLANK PAGE]

OPTION A: MEDIEVAL HISTORY

SPECIAL TOPIC 1: NORMAN CONQUEST AND EXPANSION 1050–1153

Study the sources below and then answer the questions which follow.

Source A: from William of Malmesbury, *Chronicles of the Kings of England,* written in the twelfth century.

Observing this, William gave a signal to his troops, that, pretending to flee, they should withdraw from the field. By this means, the solid formation of the English opened for the purpose of cutting down the fleeing enemy and thus brought upon itself swift destruction; for the Normans, facing about, attacked them, thus disordered, and compelled them to flee . . . But some of the English, getting possession of high ground, drove back the Normans, who in the heat of pursuit were struggling up the slope. By hurling their javelins and rolling down stones on them as they stood below, the English easily destroyed these Normans to a man. Besides, by a short passage with which the English were acquainted, they avoided a deep ditch and trod underfoot such a multitude of their enemies that the heaps of bodies made the hollow level with the plain. This alternating victory, first of one side and then of the other, continued so long as Harold lived to check the retreat; but when he fell, his brain pierced by an arrow, the flight of the English ceased not until night.

Source B: from *The Anglo-Saxon Chronicle, c* 1085.

If anyone would know what manner of man King William was, the glory that he obtained, and of how many lands he was lord, then will we describe him as we have known him, we who had looked upon him and who once lived at his court. This King William . . . was a very wise and great man, and more honoured and more powerful than any of his predecessors. He was mild to those good men who loved God, but severe beyond measure to those who stood against him. He founded a noble monastery [Battle Abbey] on the spot where God permitted him to conquer England and he established monks in it, and he made it very rich. In his days the great monastery at Canterbury was built, and many others also throughout England; moreover, this land was filled with monks who lived after the rule of St. Benedict; and such was the state of religion in his days that all who would, might observe the rules of their respective orders.

Source C: from Jim Bradbury, *The Battle of Hastings* (1998).

William punished the region with the most harsh of all his harsh measures in England, the harrying of the north. Harrying as a punishment was not new in England, but William's was so severe as to be long remembered . . . The conqueror sought out any rebel, and any who got in the way. His troops spread over a great distance, combing woodland and remote areas, leaving no hiding place unearthed. He wanted the whole region north of the Humber to be deprived of food. Houses and crops were destroyed, any living creature that crossed the path of William's troops was slaughtered till a great band of ashes and waste spread over Yorkshire . . . William's reign was hardly a happy one. At no time was he free from cares . . . within a decade he had obliterated the higher ranks of the Old English nobility. By the time of the Conqueror's death, the greater nobility in England was of continental descent.

Source D: a photograph of a Norman Motte and Bailey castle in Inverurie, known as the Bass.

Page four

Source E: from Fiona Watson, *Scotland: a History* (2001).

In Scotland, national legislation did exist, but kings of Scots knew better than to tamper with all the existing regional law. However, they did exert stricter control over much of Scotland through the formal establishment of sheriffdoms, most of which were in place by the mid-twelfth century. The sheriff was the key royal official at a local level, responsible for taxes necessary to maintain the royal household and national government and of course administering royal justice to the local population . . . However, the main legacy of David I was perhaps less his secular administration reforms . . . and more the fact that he actively encouraged the introduction to Scotland of a new . . . reformed monastic order. This marked a new phase in the economic, as well as spiritual, development of Western Europe.

[END OF SOURCES FOR SPECIAL TOPIC 1]

SPECIAL TOPIC 1: NORMAN CONQUEST AND EXPANSION 1050–1153

Answer *all* of the following questions.

Marks

1. How fully does **Source A** explain the Norman victory at the Battle of Hastings?
Use the source and recalled knowledge. **6**

2. Compare the views in **Sources B** and **C** of William's dealings with his English subjects after the Battle of Hastings in 1066.
Compare the sources overall and in detail. **5**

3. How fully do **Sources A**, **B** and **C** show the success of the Norman conquest of England?
*Use **Sources A**, **B** and **C** and recalled knowledge.* **8**

4. How useful is **Source D** in demonstrating the Normanisation of Scotland by David I?
In reaching a conclusion you should refer to:
• *the origin and possible purpose of the source;*
• *the content of the source;*
• *recalled knowledge.* **5**

5. How typical was the Scottish experience of the wider Norman achievement in Europe in the eleventh and twelfth centuries?
*Use **Source E** and recalled knowledge.* **6**

(30)

[END OF QUESTIONS ON SPECIAL TOPIC 1]

SPECIAL TOPIC 2: THE CRUSADES 1096–1204

Study the sources below and then answer the questions which follow.

Source A: from a letter written by Pope Gregory VII, written in 1074.

The person who brings this letter came to Rome to visit us on his recent return from Constantinople. He repeated what we had heard from many others, that a pagan race had overcome the Christians and with horrible cruelty had devastated everything almost to the walls of Constantinople, and were now governing the conquered lands . . . and that they had slain many thousands of Christians as if they were but sheep. If we love God and wish to be recognised as Christians, we should be filled with grief at the misfortune of this great empire and the murder of so many Christians. But simply to grieve is not our whole duty . . . Know, therefore, that we are trusting in the mercy of God and in the power of His might and that we are making preparations to send aid to the Christian empire . . . Therefore we beg you by the faith in which you are united through Christ . . . that you be moved to proper compassion by the wounds and blood of your brethren and the danger of the empire and that, for the sake of Christ, you undertake the difficult task of bringing aid to your brethren. Send messengers to us at once to inform us of what God may inspire you to do in this matter.

Source B: Peter the Hermit leads the People's Crusade, from a fourteenth century manuscript.

Source C: an account of the battle of Antioch, from the *Deeds of the Franks*, written *c.* 1100-1101.

Then six battle lines were formed from the forces within the city. In the first line, that is at the very head, was Hugh the Great with the Franks and the Count of Flanders; in the second, Duke Godfrey with his army; in the third was Robert the Norman with his knights; in the fourth, carrying with him the Lance of the Saviour, was the Bishop of Puy . . . The Turks, however, engaged them in battle and by shooting killed many of our men. They began to go forth from both sides and to surround our men on all sides, hurling, shooting and wounding them.

Then . . . there came out from the mountains, also, countless armies with white horses, whose standards were all white. And so, when our leaders saw this army, they were entirely ignorant as to what it was, and who they were, until they recognised the aid of Christ, among whose leaders was St. George . . . This is to be believed, for many of our men saw it . . . The Turks and the Persians in their turn cried out. Thereupon, we invoked the Living and True God and charged against them, and in the name of Jesus Christ and of the Holy Sepulchre we began the battle, and, God helping, we overcame them. But the terrified Turks took to flight.

Source D: from W. B. Bartlett, *God Wills It* (1999).

Weakened, as they no doubt were, it appears that they still made an impressive sight. Kerbogha, when he saw the army, somewhat belatedly asked for a truce. His approaches were ignored ... Ignoring the Turkish firestorm the Franks pressed forward ... The Turks fell back ... and it is now that the weakness of the Muslim unity at this point in history was exposed. It was split by petty internal rivalries; it lacked unity and cohesion ... Many Muslim leaders were inspired by the desire for personal gain rather than any sense of religious or political unity and many of them still seriously underestimated the threat posed by the Crusade ... A significant number of Kerbogha's Emirs feared him. Some believed that if he were to defeat the Crusade, his power would become absolute. Fearful of their own position many decided to flee with their forces, leaving Kerbogha to his fate.

Source E: from Zoë Oldenbourg, *The Crusades* (1998).

Once again Richard negotiated and in the most courteous terms. What Richard offered Saladin was the setting up of the Kingdom of Jerusalem as a Muslim protectorate. Henry of Champagne as king would become a vassal of the Sultan and fight for him against his enemies. In Jerusalem, Christians should have possession of the Holy Sepulchre and free access to the Holy Places. Richard signed a treaty with Saladin. There was an exchange of civilities which says less about the spirit of mutual understanding between them than about their haste to put an end to fighting. For Richard, who was no diplomat, it was a matter of saving face ... The duke of Burgundy and his French barons did not approve of this policy and were disgusted to find themselves unwilling accomplices in what they regarded as a shameful desertion.

[END OF SOURCES FOR SPECIAL TOPIC 2]

SPECIAL TOPIC 2: THE CRUSADES 1096–1204

Answer *all* of the following questions.

Marks

1. How fully does **Source A** describe the Roman Church's motives in calling the First Crusade?
   Use the source and recalled knowledge.　　　　　　　　　　　　　　　　　　**6**

2. How useful is **Source B** as evidence of the range of people who followed Peter the Hermit during the People's Crusade?
   In reaching a conclusion you should refer to:
   * *the origin and possible purpose of the source;*
   * *the content of the source;*
   * *recalled knowledge.*　　　　　　　　　　　　　　　　　　　　　　　　**5**

3. Compare the reasons given in **Sources C** and **D** for the defeat of the Muslim army at the battle of Antioch.
   Compare the sources overall and in detail.　　　　　　　　　　　　　　**5**

4. Why was the First Crusade such a success for the Crusaders?
   *Use **Sources A**, **C** and **D** and recalled knowledge.*　　　　　　　　　**8**

5. How accurately does **Source E** illustrate the decline of the crusading ideal by 1204?
   Use the source and recalled knowledge.　　　　　　　　　　　　　　　**6**

(30)

[END OF QUESTIONS ON SPECIAL TOPIC 2]

OPTION B: EARLY MODERN HISTORY

SPECIAL TOPIC 3: SCOTLAND 1689–1715

Study the sources below and then answer the questions which follow.

Source A: from Keith Brown, *Kingdom or Province? Scotland and the Regal Union* (1992).

The last year of William's reign was overshadowed by the additional problem of the death in 1701 of Princess Anne's last surviving child, the Duke of Gloucester. As Anne was William's only heir this left the succession vulnerable, especially when Louis XIV recognised Anne's Jacobite half brother. Consequently, the English Parliament passed the Act of Settlement, regulating the succession and making Sophia, the electress of Hanover, heir to Anne. Scottish intentions were ignored in making this decision, which was seen by the Scottish Parliament as another example of English arrogance. William's own unexpected death in March 1702 left the crown in the hands of an unhealthy, childless woman, and made a resolution of the succession urgent.

Source B: William Patterson's vision of a Scottish Colony, written in the 1690s.

The time and expense of navigation to China, Japan and the Spice Islands, and the East Indies, will be reduced by more than half, and the consumption of European commodities will soon be more than doubled. Trade will increase trade, and money will make money, and the trading world shall need no more work for their people, but rather need people for their work.

Source C: from Broun, Finlay & Lynch (eds), *Image and Identity* (1998).

By the end of the 1704 session the Hanoverian succession had still not been secured. Ideas of a federal union with England had been put forward as well as further reform of the Scottish constitution. Nevertheless, the English response to the drawn out Scottish problem was precise. Under the terms of the Aliens Act 1705, Scots would be treated as Aliens in England and Scottish exports would be banned from English markets . . . In addition, there were threats of an invading English military force into Scotland. Uncertainty about the succession, a possible Jacobite restoration to the Scottish throne and most importantly the strategic safety of England's northern border during the war of the Spanish Succession, ensured that a resolution of the instability of Scottish affairs had to be found.

Source D: from a speech made by Seton of Pitmedden, on the first Article of the Treaty, 2 November 1706.

In general, I may point out, that by this Union, we'll have access to all the advantages in commerce the English enjoy: we'll be able, with good government, to improve our national product, for the benefit of the whole island; and we'll have our Liberty, Property and Religion, secured under the protection of one Sovereign, and one Parliament of Great Britain . . .

Let us therefore, My Lord, after all these considerations approve this Article: and when the whole Treaty shall be duly examined and ratified, I am hopeful that this Parliament will return their most dutiful thanks to Her Majesty for her royal endeavours in promoting a lasting Union between both nations.

Source E: from a petition to the Duke of Queensberry, 1706.

There is a Treaty with England laid before your Grace and the honourable estates of parliament, which overturns the very constitution of this Ancient Kingdom, suppresses our monarchy, and extinguishes our Parliament. This Treaty subjects all our fundamental rights, overthrows our religion and liberty, destroys the government of our Church and surrenders all that is precious to us to the will of the English in a British Parliament . . . making this Ancient Kingdom of Scotland just another part of England . . .

We do therefore with all our right hearted countrymen, humbly ask your Grace that no union be hastily entered into with England . . . And that the Treaty agreed on between the Commissioners for Scotland and the Commissioners for England may be rejected.

[END OF SOURCES FOR SPECIAL TOPIC 3]

SPECIAL TOPIC 3: SCOTLAND 1689–1715

Answer *all* of the following questions.

Marks

1. How important were the issues raised in **Source A** in causing poor relations between Scotland and England between 1701 and 1705?
   Use the source and recalled knowledge.　　6

2. How useful is **Source B** as evidence of the reasons for setting up the Darien scheme?
   In reaching a conclusion you should refer to:
   * *the origin and possible purpose of the source;*
   * *the content of the source;*
   * *recalled knowledge.*　　5

3. How fully does **Source C** explain why England wanted an incorporating Union?
   Use the source and recalled knowledge.　　6

4. Compare the attitudes towards Union revealed in **Sources D** and **E**.
   Compare the sources overall and in detail.　　5

5. How far do **Sources A**, **C** and **D** explain the reasons why the Scottish Parliament passed the Act of Union?
   *Use **Sources A, C** and **D** and recalled knowledge.*　　8

　　(30)

[END OF QUESTIONS ON SPECIAL TOPIC 3]

SPECIAL TOPIC 4: THE ATLANTIC SLAVE TRADE

Study the sources below and then answer the questions which follow.

Source A: from Eric Williams, *"Slavery, Industrialisation and Abolition"* in D. Northrup (ed), *The Atlantic Slave Trade* (2002).

Britain was accumulating great wealth from the triangular trade. The demand for manufactured goods from that trade inevitably increased production. This industrial expansion required finance. What man was better able to afford the ready capital than a West Indian sugar planter or a Liverpool slave trader?

In June, 1783, the Prime Minister, Lord North, complimented the Quaker opponents of the slave trade on their humanity, but regretted that its abolition was an impossibility, as the trade had become necessary to almost every nation in Europe. Slave traders and sugar planters rubbed their hands in glee. The West Indian colonies were still the darlings of the Empire, the most precious jewels in the British crown.

Source B: from Olaudah Equiano, *Narrative of his Life* (1789).

One day, two of my wearied countrymen who were chained together, preferring death to such a life of misery, somehow made through the nettings and jumped into the sea. Immediately another quite dejected fellow, who on account of his illness was allowed to be out of irons, also followed their example, and I believe many more would very soon have done the same if they had not been prevented by the ship's crew. Two of the wretches were drowned, but they got the other and afterwards flogged him unmercifully for thus attempting to prefer death to slavery. In this manner we continued to undergo more hardships than I can now relate, hardships which are inseparable from this accursed trade.

Source C: from Earl Leslie Griggs, *Thomas Clarkson* (1936).

The value of Clarkson's services to the abolition of the slave trade is inestimable. Almost single-handed, he obtained the necessary witnesses for the various parliamentary investigations of the slave trade. He provided Wilberforce with the convincing evidence which made Wilberforce's speeches so graphic and appealing. He had spread propaganda from one end of the country to the other. No task was too great, no labour too small. Let it be remembered that Clarkson, the first great propagandist, was more instrumental than anyone else in discovering and presenting to the English people the true picture of the slave trade.

Source D: from a letter to Wilberforce by Samuel Hoare, February 1792.

The members of the Church of England have put forward an idea that the Dissenters wish for a revolution, and that the abolition of the slave trade is somewhat connected with it. I hope this has no foundation. However, some enquiries of Mr Clarkson have added to this belief. In some letters he declares that he is a friend to the French Revolution. If I knew where he was, I would write to him on the subject.

A moment's reflection must convince him that there is too much reason to fear that his own private thoughts will be considered an opinion of our committee. I hope you will lose no time in giving him a hint upon this subject, or our cause will be severely injured.

Source E: from Hugh Thomas, *The Slave Trade* (1997).

But there was opposition. Bamber Gascoyne even said that he was "persuaded that the slave trade might be made a much greater source of revenue and riches . . . than it was at present".

His fellow Member for Liverpool, Lord Penrhyn, said that, were the Commons to vote for abolition, "they actually would strike at seventy million pounds worth of property, they would ruin the colonies, and by destroying an essential nursery of seamen, give up British control of the sea at a single stroke".

The members of Parliament for London also strongly opposed abolition. Alderman Sawbridge opposed Wilberforce on the ground that abolition would not serve Africans. "If they could not be sold as slaves, they would be butchered and executed at home."

[END OF SOURCES FOR SPECIAL TOPIC 4]

SPECIAL TOPIC 4: THE ATLANTIC SLAVE TRADE

Answer *all* of the following questions.

Marks

1. How accurately does **Source A** reflect the attitude of British governments to the slave trade in the eighteenth century?
   Use the source and recalled knowledge.　　**6**

2. How useful is **Source B** as evidence of the slave experience on board ship?
   In reaching a conclusion you should refer to:
   * *the origin and possible purpose of the source;*
   * *the content of the source;*
   * *recalled knowledge.*　　**5**

3. How fully does **Source C** identify the methods used by the abolitionists to promote their cause?
   Use the source and recalled knowledge.　　**6**

4. To what extent does the evidence in **Source D** support **Source C**'s assessment of Clarkson's contribution to the abolition of the slave trade?
   Compare the sources overall and in detail.　　**5**

5. How fully do **Sources A**, **D** and **E** illustrate the difficulties faced by the abolitionists in their campaign?
   *Use **Sources A, D** and **E** and recalled knowledge.*　　**8**

　　(30)

[END OF QUESTIONS ON SPECIAL TOPIC 4]

SPECIAL TOPIC 5: THE AMERICAN REVOLUTION

Study the sources below and then answer the questions which follow.

Source A: from a letter sent by John Dickinson, a farmer from Pennsylvania, to the inhabitants of the British colonies, May 1774.

Great Britain follows a policy of suppressing the freedom of America by a military force, to be supported by money taken out of our pockets . . . The people in Britain are misled into a belief that we are in a state of rebellion . . . The minister addressing the House of Commons calls the stoppage of the port of Boston "a punishment inflicted on those who have disobeyed Parliament". Surely you cannot doubt at this time, my countrymen, but that the people of Massachusetts Bay are suffering in a cause common to us all.

I offer some observations concerning the measures that may be most effective in the present emergency. Other nations have fought for their liberty, and have judged the prize worth the price that was paid for it. These colonies need not go as far as that. So dependent is Great Britain on us for supplies, that heaven seems to have placed in our hands the means of an effective, yet peaceable resistance. A general agreement between these colonies on non-importation and non-exportation faithfully observed would certainly be successful.

Source B: from Peter D. G. Thomas, *Revolution in America* (1992).

Of immediate significance was the misunderstanding by Congress of British opinion, and the American belief in the effectiveness of a refusal to trade with Britain. Although Congress had rejected military action, it had nevertheless deliberately challenged Britain. Congress was bluffing, confident that Britain would again give ground, as in 1766 and 1770. This time Britain did not do so, and called the colonial bluff. The delegates at the Second Continental Congress in May 1775 faced an armed conflict which most of them did not want. Hostilities had accidentally already commenced. The war of independence was the result of a political miscalculation by a Congress that had chosen to avoid a military conflict and yet blundered into one.

Source C: from David F. Burg, *The American Revolution* (2001).

The Continental Congress met at the State House in Philadelphia, where delegates began to consider the issue of American independence from Great Britain. Already in early January (1776) New Hampshire became the first of the colonies to establish an independent government, whereas the Maryland Convention . . . followed the stance that avoided any support of independence for the colonies. At the same time, however, the drive towards independence received a huge boost with the publication in Philadelphia of Thomas Paine's *Common Sense*, which argued that efforts at reconciliation were useless and strongly urged creation of an independent, continental republic . . . Widely distributed and read, *Common Sense* favourably impressed and persuaded not only such leaders as Adams and Washington, but also tens of thousands of their fellow Americans.

Source D: from a diary entry by Christopher Marshall, 17 January 1778, Valley Forge.

My mind seems anxiously concerned on account of our distressed friends and acquaintances with our brave General Washington, as he and his army are now obliged to encounter all the severity of this cold weather, as they with him are living out in the woods with little shelter. Our poor friends in town [Philadelphia] have need of fuel and other necessaries, while the British supporters, under the protection of that savage monster Howe, are revelling in luxury and drunkenness, without any feelings for the distress of their (once happy) bleeding country.

Source E: from the *New York Journal*, 18 May 1778.

At last we have news from France that Congress has concluded a treaty of alliance with the King of the French. His Most Christian Majesty guarantees the independence, sovereignty, liberties, and all the possessions of the United States of America; and Congress, on its part, guarantees all the dominions of the French king in the West Indies. No monopoly of our trade is desired. It is left open to us whom we choose to trade with. We are, moreover, to be assisted generously with all kinds of supplies . . . The Treaties were signed on the sixth of February.

[END OF SOURCES FOR SPECIAL TOPIC 5]

SPECIAL TOPIC 5: THE AMERICAN REVOLUTION

Answer *all* of the following questions.

Marks

1. How fully does **Source A** identify the reasons for the colonial challenge to British control of America by 1774?
   Use the source and recalled knowledge.   **7**

2. Compare the views expressed in **Sources A** and **B** on colonial actions after the passing of the Coercive Acts in 1774.
   Compare the sources overall and in detail.   **5**

3. How fully do **Sources A**, **B**, and **C** illustrate the issues that led the Americans to declare independence from Britain in 1776?
   *Use **Sources A**, **B** and **C** and recalled knowledge.*   **8**

4. How valuable is **Source D** to an understanding of Washington's difficulties in fighting the war against Britain?
   In reaching a conclusion you should refer to:
   * *the origin and possible purpose of the source;*
   * *the content of the source;*
   * *recalled knowledge.*   **5**

5. How important was foreign intervention in the outcome of the war?
   *Use **Source E** and recalled knowledge.*   **5**

                                                                                              (30)

[END OF QUESTIONS ON SPECIAL TOPIC 5]

OPTION C: LATER MODERN HISTORY

SPECIAL TOPIC 6: PATTERNS OF MIGRATION: SCOTLAND 1830s–1930s

Study the sources below and then answer the questions which follow.

Source A: from Danny McGowan, "Scotland, Sectarianism, and the Irish diaspora", in *Frontline Online*, the website of the International Socialist Movement, Issue 4, 22 October 2001.

Immigrants meet racism rather than create it. Large-scale immigration did not cause anti-Irish racism, but it gave a focus for existing hostility. General contempt for the poor was reinforced by racial stereotypes. The Irish migrated to an urban squalor where drink offered a temporary escape, yet found themselves blamed for causing the squalor through their own drunkenness. Their communities were criminalised and subject to excessive police surveillance. Though the idea of an Irish "threat" still figures in some historical explanations, they were "despised rather than actively feared".

Source B: from the *Ayr Advertiser*, 1849.

The influence of the Irish on older people, though quite considerable, must be small when compared with their influence on the young population. Mixing as they must with Irish of their own age, they will, at the most easily influenced time of their lives, receive impressions from their vicious Irish companions. In future years this will not either promote the private welfare of young Scots or that of Scotland. While we earnestly hope for the recovery of Ireland from her degraded position so that this plague of immigrants in time may be halted, we are called upon to another task – that of meeting the evil as it already exists by the weapons of religion and education.

Source C: from a letter sent by Godfrey McKinnon in Australia to John McDonald in Uist, 1864.

I had very hard work of it the first three years that I was in this country but now I can take it a little easier. I have done very well for all the time I have been here, more than if I had been in Skye for the rest of my life, even if I were to live for fifty years or more. I have got a beautiful piece of country and first rate stock of sheep, cattle and horses. I have gone to great expense with my sheep purchases – imported rams. It will pay me very well in a few years. I had a splendid clip of wool this season and I expect an even better clip next season.

Source D: from a report by the Immigration Agent for Victoria, Australia, 1853.

I do not consider that the inhabitants of the Islands of Scotland are well suited to the wants and needs of this colony. Their total ignorance of the English language makes it difficult to get employment for them, while their laziness and extremely filthy habits have not made a good impression on the British people already here. It would be better if such immigration was restricted at least, since these wretches have little of worth to offer this society. Indeed, it cannot be argued other than that their arrival is having a most unwelcome and detrimental effect on the inhabitants of this colony.

Source E: from Jenni Calder, *Scots in Canada* (2004).

The individual experiences of emigrant Scots varied, but even those who felt most positively about their new lives in Canada did not necessarily want to lose their Scottishness, nor did it seem becoming Canadian required that. Shinty came to Canada with the Scots, and out of it was born ice hockey. Indeed, as the many Scottish societies suggest, the more integrated these migrants became, the more important it became not just to preserve a Scottish identity but to maintain links with other Scots.

An important part of the role of Scottish societies in Canada was to look after their own, in a way that might not have seemed appropriate or necessary in the old country. Many Highland societies, as well as promoting Highland music and dancing, became the focus of Highland sporting activities. A piece in the *Celtic Monthly* of July 1893 states that "the national sentiment is stimulated because of the manly exercises of the Highland games of the old home being kept alive". These events were mainly for those who identified themselves as being of Scottish origin, but they were also spectacles that could hardly fail to have an impact on whatever community hosted them.

[END OF SOURCES FOR SPECIAL TOPIC 6]

SPECIAL TOPIC 6: PATTERNS OF MIGRATION: SCOTLAND 1830s–1930s

Marks

Answer *all* of the following questions.

1. How accurate is the explanation in **Source A** for anti-Irish attitudes in nineteenth-century Scotland?
   Use the source and recalled knowledge.   6

2. To what extent does the evidence in **Source B** support the views expressed in **Source A**?
   Compare the sources overall and in detail.   5

3. How useful is **Source C** as evidence of the success of Scottish emigrants in their new lands?
   In reaching a conclusion you should refer to:
   * *the origin and possible purpose of the source;*
   * *the content of the source;*
   * *recalled knowledge.*   5

4. How typical are the views expressed in **Source D** of the attitudes towards Scots in the lands to which they emigrated in the nineteenth century?
   Use the source and recalled knowledge.   6

5. How fully do **Sources C, D** and **E** illustrate the experiences of Scots emigrants between the 1830s and 1930s?
   *Use **Sources C, D** and **E** and recalled knowledge.*   8

                                                                       (30)

[END OF QUESTIONS ON SPECIAL TOPIC 6]

SPECIAL TOPIC 7: APPEASEMENT AND THE ROAD TO WAR, TO 1939

Study the sources below and then answer the questions which follow.

Source A: from Ian Kershaw, *Making Friends with Hitler: Lord Londonderry and Britain's Road to War* (2004).

The German ambassador in London read out to Eden the German memorandum justifying the remilitarisation of the Rhineland and blaming the Franco-Soviet treaty for the violation of Locarno. It also put forward Hitler's skilfully devised offer – certain to calm public opinion in Britain – to reach new agreements. These would involve non aggression pacts for a duration of 25 years with his neighbours, a new demilitarised zone now on both sides of the border, a western air force agreement and German re-entry to the League of Nations.

Prime Minister Baldwin's government was only too aware that public opinion was opposed to any risk of war and was largely supportive of Germany. It was even more aware of British military weakness. So it left the French in no doubt that Britain was unwilling to take any steps that would risk military involvement with Germany.

Source B: from a letter by Douglas Reed, foreign correspondent of *The Times*, to his editor, March 1938.

I believe it is already too late. Britain's military defeat is coming. I saw the German fighting machine enter Austria. It is terrifying. Indeed worse than anything I imagined, and you will realise that is saying a great deal . . . In my wildest nightmares I had not imagined anything so perfectly organised . . . The vital thing to remember is they want to destroy Britain.

In May 1936, I wrote some articles about these coming dangers which you did not use at the time because you thought they were too alarmist.

Source C: a cartoon by David Low, published in the *Evening Standard*, 10 September 1938. The figure in the soldier's pocket represents Henlein, the Sudeten Nazi leader. The figure holding the lamb represents Benes, the leader of Czechoslovakia.

"HE ONLY WANTS TO LIE DOWN WITH YOUR LAMB"

Source D: from a speech by Neville Chamberlain in the House of Commons, 3 October 1938.

I think it is very essential not to forget certain things when the terms of the Munich agreement are being considered. All the elements were present for the outbreak of a conflict which might have brought about the catastrophe. In the Sudetenland, we had extremists on both sides ready to work up and provoke incidents. We had considerable quantities of arms which were not confined to regular armies. Therefore, it was essential that we should quickly reach a conclusion, so that this painful and difficult operation of transfer might be carried out at the earliest possible moment.

Before giving a verdict upon the Munich agreement, we should do well to avoid describing it as a personal or a national triumph for anyone. The real triumph is that it has shown that representatives of four great powers can find it possible to agree on a way of carrying out a difficult and delicate operation by discussion instead of by force of arms. Thereby, they have averted a catastrophe which would have ended civilisation as we have known it. The relief at our escape from this great peril of war has, I think, everywhere been mingled in this country with a profound feeling of sympathy.

I have nothing to be ashamed of.

Source E: from a speech by the Labour leader, Clement Attlee, in the House of Commons, 3 October 1938.

We all feel relief that war has not come this time. Every one of us has been passing through days of anxiety. We cannot, however, feel that peace has been established, but that we have nothing but an armistice in a state of war. We have been unable to go in for carefree rejoicing. We have felt that we are in the midst of a tragedy. We have felt humiliation. This has not been a victory for reason and humanity. It has been a victory for brute force. At every stage of the proceedings, there have been time limits laid down by the owner and ruler of armed force. The terms have not been negotiated; they have been terms laid down as ultimata. We have seen today a gallant, civilised and democratic people betrayed and handed over to a ruthless dictatorship. We have seen something more. We have seen the cause of democracy, which is, in our view, the cause of civilisation and humanity, receive a terrible defeat.

[END OF SOURCES FOR SPECIAL TOPIC 7]

SPECIAL TOPIC 7: APPEASEMENT AND THE ROAD TO WAR, TO 1939

Answer *all* of the following questions.

Marks

1. To what extent does **Source A** explain why Britain did not take strong action against Germany immediately after the remilitarisation of the Rhineland?
   Use the source and recalled knowledge.

   6

2. How fully does **Source B** illustrate British opinion towards the Anschluss?
   Use the source and recalled knowledge.

   6

3. How valuable is **Source C** as evidence of British attitudes towards the crisis over Czechoslovakia in 1938?
   In reaching a conclusion you should refer to:
   * *the origin and possible purpose of the source;*
   * *the content of the source;*
   * *recalled knowledge.*

   5

4. Compare the views expressed in **Sources D** and **E** on the Munich agreement.
   Compare the sources overall and in detail.

   5

5. To what extent was the British policy of appeasement justified in view of the issues facing Britain in the 1930s?
   *Use **Sources B, C** and **D** and recalled knowledge.*

   8

[END OF QUESTIONS ON SPECIAL TOPIC 7]

(30)

SPECIAL TOPIC 8: THE ORIGINS AND DEVELOPMENT OF THE COLD WAR 1945–1985

Study the sources below and then answer the questions which follow.

Source A: from the Resolution of the Council of Ministers of the German Democratic Republic, 12 August 1961.

The desire for revenge has intensified in West Germany, with increasing territorial claims against the German Democratic Republic and neighbouring states. This is closely tied to accelerated rearmament and the acquisition of nuclear weapons by West Germany. The Adenauer administration is making preparations for civil war against the GDR. West German and West Berlin espionage headquarters are systematically putting citizens of the GDR under pressure and organising the smuggling of human beings.

For all these reasons, the Council of Ministers of the GDR is taking the following measures to secure peace in Europe and protect the GDR . . . A border control will be introduced at the borders to the GDR, including the borders with West Berlin. Borders to West Berlin will be sufficiently guarded and effectively controlled to prevent subversive activities from the West.

Source B: from an address by the Vice-President of the United States, Lyndon B. Johnson, to the Berlin Parliament, 19 August 1961.

This crisis has arisen because of a massive fact of history. The free men of Germany – both here and in West Germany – have succeeded since the end of the war beyond our most optimistic hopes. I am not referring only to their economic success, which all the world knows and admires. They succeeded in far more important ways. They have built a vital democratic life . . . They have played a great constructive role in making a united Europe. They are now coming to play a major role on the world scene.

Meanwhile, in East Germany, there has been a terrible and tragic failure. Despite the use of force and propaganda, the Communists have not been able to create a life to which men can commit their talents, their faith, and the future of their children.

Make no mistake. This fact of history is well understood in the Kremlin. What they are trying to do now is to place barbed wire, bayonets, and tanks against the forces of history.

Source C: from J. Young and J. Kent, *International Relations since 1945* (2004).

The risks that were run during the Cuban Missile Crisis, and indeed the reasons for running them, have probably been overstated. At the end of the day neither leader was likely to have ordered a major nuclear strike for the sake of strategic benefits that were more apparent than real. Yet there were serious risks . . .

There was the danger of local commanders seizing the initiative and dragging their superiors into a conflict they would have wanted at all costs to avoid. Not only did the US Navy clash with the Soviets, but a local commander in Cuba, acting on his own authority, shot down an American U2 spy plane on 25th October. In addition, General Tommy Power, the head of the US Strategic Air Command, placed his forces on DEFCON 2 (Defence Condition 2) and prepared for immediate action without consulting the White House.

The flaws in the decision-making process and the chain of command could have led to a nuclear clash because of the level of brinkmanship, despite the politicians' desire to avoid any such conflict.

Source D: from the Action Programme of the Communist Party of Czechoslovakia, 5 April 1968.

Comrades

We are not changing our basic beliefs. We want to develop to the utmost in this country an advanced socialist society, which will be economically, technologically, and socially highly advanced. It will be socially and nationally just, and democratically organised.

We want to start building up a new, strongly democratic model of a socialist society which will fully correspond to Czechoslovak conditions.

Our own experiences and Marxist knowledge lead us jointly to the conclusion that these aims cannot be achieved along the old paths . . .

We want to set new forces of socialist life in motion, to make possible a much more effective social system and to demonstrate fully the advantages of socialism.

Source E: from E. J Hobsbawm, *The Age of Extremes* (1995).

The Action Programme of the Czechoslovak Communist Party might or might not have been – just – acceptable to the Soviet Union. However, the cohesion, perhaps the very existence, of the East European Soviet bloc seemed to be at stake, as the "Prague Spring" revealed and increased the cracks within it. Hard-line regimes without mass support, such as Poland and East Germany, feared internal destabilisation from the Czech example, which they criticised bitterly. As a result, the Russians decided to overthrow the Prague regime by military force.

This held the Soviet bloc together for another twenty years, but henceforth only by the threat of Soviet military intervention. In the last twenty years of the Soviet bloc, even the leadership of the ruling communist parties appeared to have lost any real belief in what they were doing.

[END OF SOURCES FOR SPECIAL TOPIC 8]

SPECIAL TOPIC 8: THE ORIGINS AND DEVELOPMENT OF THE COLD WAR 1945–1985

Answer *all* of the following questions.

Marks

1. How useful is **Source A** as evidence of East Germany's attitude towards West Berlin in 1961?
   In reaching a conclusion you should refer to:
   • *the origin and possible purpose of the source;*
   • *the content of the source;*
   • *recalled knowledge.*   **5**

2. Compare the attitudes towards the Berlin Crisis of 1961 expressed in **Sources A** and **B**.
   Compare the sources overall and in detail.   **5**

3. How accurate is the assessment in **Source C** of the risks of conflict during the Cuban Missile Crisis of 1962?
   Use the source and recalled knowledge.   **6**

4. To what extent does **Source D** explain the aims of the reform movement in Czechoslovakia in 1968?
   Use the source and recalled knowledge.   **6**

5. How fully did differences in ideology explain the reasons for tension between the Superpowers during the Cold War?
   *Use **Sources A, C** and **E** and recalled knowledge.*   **8**

[END OF QUESTIONS ON SPECIAL TOPIC 8]

(30)

SPECIAL TOPIC 9: IRELAND 1900–1985: A DIVIDED IDENTITY

Study the sources below and then answer the questions which follow.

Source A: from a speech by the Irish Nationalist MP, John Dillon, in the House of Commons, 15 April 1912.

We look forward to this Home Rule Bill with hope and enthusiasm. The Ireland we look forward to under this Bill is an Ireland which will become self-supporting and will be ready to take its share in all the burdens of the British Empire. Ireland will do so, not as an unwilling slave, but as a willing partner. We will take a willing share, not only by contributing to the financial burdens of the Empire, but we shall contribute what is greater than that, namely the bravery of our sons.

I tell the men of Ulster, and the Protestants of Ireland, that, if they will only join us in the great effort to realise this dream, they will find that the day on which they make up their minds to trust their own countrymen will be the happiest day in the history of Ireland.

Source B: from a speech by the Ulster Unionist MP, William Moore, in the House of Commons, 15 April 1912.

I want to say what my policy is. I say solemnly here that, as long as they have a drop of blood in their veins, Ulster men will do their best to make the government in Ulster by the Nationalist Party impossible. We shall leave no stone unturned, but do our best to make every effort to carry out that policy successfully. We pledged our lives to this policy the other day in Belfast.

If you are going to plant Home Rule, you cannot do it until you have wiped us out, and the blood will be on your hands, and not on ours.

If, without my consent, you transfer my allegiance to a new Constitution proposed without my consent; if you propose to sell me into a political slavery under the new Constitution you are setting up, I say that I do not regard it as rebelling to resist that to the best of my ability and, please God, I shall do it.

Source C: from F. S. L. Lyons, *Ireland since the Famine* (1973).

All the passion and determination which Sinn Féin had been able to mobilise against the threat of military service was thrown behind it in the general election of 1918. It did not matter that many Sinn Féin candidates were in prison, or that their manifesto was heavily censored. On the contrary, these government actions were an advantage.

Sinn Féin's message was a restatement of the republican ideal, which was to be achieved by a four-point policy. First, they would withdraw from Westminster: second, to make use of any means available to weaken the power of Britain to control Ireland by military force: third, the establishment of a constituent assembly as the supreme authority for Ireland: finally, to appeal to the Peace Conference at Versailles to establish Ireland as an independent nation. Such a programme proved irresistible.

Source D: from a speech by Count George N. Plunkett in the Dail Eireann during a debate on the Anglo-Irish Treaty, 19 December 1921.

We should reject this Treaty because it goes against the conscience of the Irish people.

We are told that our national liberties will be secured by handing them over to the authority of the British Government. British rule was rejected, not only by our generation, but by past generations of fighting men. We are now told that we must swear an oath of allegiance to the English king, and that this is the only means by which we will achieve our liberty.

I am not going to abandon the cause to which I have devoted my life. I am no more an enemy of peace than Arthur Griffith, but I will never sacrifice the independence of Ireland simply to stop the fighting. We have taken an oath of loyalty to the Republic. Are we going to take a false oath now to King George?

Source E: from M. Hopkinson, *Green against Green: The Irish Civil War* (1988).

The Irish Civil War revealed the gap between political reality and political desires among Irish nationalists. It was fought over the way in which the Anglo-Irish Treaty defined the new Irish state's relationship to Britain.

To the Republicans, the Treaty betrayed the commitment to an Irish republic, completely independent of Britain, leaving Ireland in effect a British dominion, although with significant powers of self-government.

To the pro-Treaty side, it was the best offer available in the circumstances. In the words of Michael Collins, it gave Ireland "freedom – not the ultimate freedom that all nations desire and develop to, but the freedom to achieve it."

Strangely, the partition of Ireland was hardly an issue at all in the war.

[END OF SOURCES FOR SPECIAL TOPIC 9]

SPECIAL TOPIC 9: IRELAND 1900–1985: A DIVIDED IDENTITY

Answer *all* of the following questions.

Marks

1. How useful is **Source A** as evidence of Irish attitudes towards the policy of Home Rule at the time?
   In reaching a conclusion you should refer to:
   - *the origin and possible purpose of the source;*
   - *the content of the source;*
   - *recalled knowledge.*   **5**

2. Compare the views on the Home Rule Bill of 1912 expressed in **Sources A** and **B**.
   Compare the sources overall and in detail.   **5**

3. How fully does **Source C** explain the reasons for the growth in support for Sinn Féin in the election of 1918?
   Use the source and recalled knowledge.   **6**

4. To what extent did the views expressed in **Source D** reflect Irish opinion towards the Peace Treaty with Britain?
   Use the source and recalled knowledge.   **6**

5. To what extent do **Sources B**, **C** and **E** illustrate the difficulties in achieving peace in Ireland between 1912 and 1922?
   *Use **Sources B, C** and **E** and recalled knowledge.*   **8**

     (30)

[END OF QUESTIONS ON SPECIAL TOPIC 9]

[END OF QUESTION PAPER]

[BLANK PAGE]

Official SQA Past Papers: Higher History 2007

[BLANK PAGE]

X044/301

NATIONAL
QUALIFICATIONS
2008

MONDAY, 26 MAY
9.00 AM – 10.20 AM

HISTORY
HIGHER
Paper 1

Answer questions on **one** Option only.

Take particular care to show clearly the Option chosen. On the **front** of the answer book, **in the top right-hand corner**, write A or B or C.

Within the Option chosen, answer **two** questions, one from Historical Study: Scottish and British and one from Historical Study: European and World.

All questions are assigned 20 marks.

Marks may be deducted for bad spelling and bad punctuation, and for writing that is difficult to read.

[BLANK PAGE]

OPTION A: MEDIEVAL HISTORY

**Answer TWO questions, one from Historical Study: Scottish and British
and one from Historical Study: European and World**

Historical Study: Scottish and British

Medieval Society

1. "In 12th Century Scotland and England, the strengths of the Feudal System considerably outweighed its weaknesses." How accurate is this view?

2. How great an impact did the regular Church have on Medieval Society?

3. To what extent can it be argued that events such as the Investiture Contest indicate that the medieval Church was more interested in politics than religion?

4. How important was the development of the Scottish economy in strengthening the powers of the Crown during the reign of David I?

5. To what extent was the dispute between Henry II and Becket a continuation of the wider struggle between Church and State?

Historical Study: European and World

EITHER

Nation and King

6. "History has judged him to be a failure." How valid is this view of the reign of King John (1199–1216)?

7. How important was the weakness of baronial opposition in the strengthening of the power of the French monarchy during the reign of Philip Augustus?

8. How successful was Louis IX in expanding the power of the French monarchy?

9. To what extent was Robert Bruce more concerned with personal ambition than with Scottish independence?

OR

Crisis of Authority

10. To what extent was the eventual French victory in the Hundred Years' War due to the contribution of Joan of Arc?

11. How important were uprisings such as the Jacquerie and the Peasants' Revolt in causing the decline of serfdom?

12. "The impact of the Black Death upon medieval society was not entirely harmful." How valid is this view?

13. To what extent did the Great Schism reduce the authority of the Church?

OPTION B: EARLY MODERN HISTORY

Answer TWO questions, one from Historical Study: Scottish and British and one from Historical Study: European and World

Historical Study: Scottish and British

EITHER

Scotland in the Age of the Reformation 1542–1603

1. How successful was the Roman Catholic Church in its attempts to reform itself before 1560?

2. How far was the death of Mary of Guise the main reason for the success of the Protestant Reformation in Scotland?

3. To what extent was Mary Queen of Scots herself to blame for the loss of her throne in 1567?

4. "Mary's forced abdication was the main reason for political instability in Scotland in the period 1567–1585." How valid is this view?

5. How significant were James VI's relations with the Church in his attempts to strengthen royal authority up to 1603?

OR

Scotland and England in the Century of Revolutions 1603–1702

6. How far were religious issues the main threat to royal authority under James VI and I?

7. How important were Charles I's financial policies in weakening his authority in the years before the Civil War?

8. "Purely a response to the attempts of Charles I to impose his religious views on Scotland." How valid is this view of the growth of the Covenanting movement?

9. To what extent was the Republic successful in overcoming its problems between 1649 and 1660?

10. How successful was the Glorious Revolution in limiting the powers of the Crown?

Historical Study: European and World

EITHER

Royal Authority in 17th and 18th Century Europe

11. How successfully did Louis XIV increase the power of the monarchy during his reign?

12. To what extent should the credit for Louis XIV's achievements be given to his ministers?

13. How far did the enlightened reforms of Frederick II lead to significant changes to life in Prussia?

14. To what extent was Joseph II himself responsible for the limited success of his reforms?

OR

The French Revolution: The Emergence of the Citizen State

15. How far were the ideas of the Enlightenment the most serious challenge to the Ancien Regime?

16. To what extent was the decision to abolish the monarchy in 1792 a result of the pressures of war?

17. How effective was the government of the Jacobin dictatorship, 1793–1794?

18. To what extent had the Ancien Regime been destroyed by 1799?

[Turn over

OPTION C: LATER MODERN HISTORY

Answer TWO questions, one from Historical Study: Scottish and British and one from Historical Study: European and World

Historical Study: Scottish and British

Britain 1850s–1979

1. To what extent was the growth of democracy in Britain after 1860 due to social and economic change?

2. How important were concerns about the extent of poverty in Britain in the Liberal Government's decision to introduce social reforms between 1906 and 1914?

3. "Their contribution during World War I was the main reason why the majority of women gained the right to vote in 1918." How valid is this view?

4. How successful was the National Government in dealing with the difficulties caused by the Depression of the 1930s?

5. **Either**

   (a) To what extent did urbanisation increase social divisions in Scotland, 1880–1939? Discuss with reference to religion, leisure and education.

   Or

   (b) "Political nationalism in Scotland only became a serious force from the 1960s onwards." How accurate is this view?

Historical Study: European and World

EITHER

The Growth of Nationalism

Germany

6. How important was Bismarck's leadership in the achievement of German unification?

7. How successful was the new German state in winning popular support during the period 1871–1914?

8. How important were weaknesses and divisions among his opponents in explaining Hitler's rise to power by 1933?

9. To what extent did the Nazis' control of Germany up to 1939 depend on their social and economic policies?

Italy

10. How significant was the military leadership of Garibaldi in the achievement of Italian unification?

11. How successful was the new Italian state in winning popular support during the period 1871–1914?

12. How important were weaknesses and divisions among his opponents in explaining Mussolini's rise to power by 1922?

13. To what extent did the Fascists' control of Italy up to 1939 depend on their social and economic policies?

[Turn over for The Large Scale State on *Page eight*

OR

The Large Scale State

The USA

14. "Economically, socially, and politically divided." How accurate is this view of American society in the 1920s?

15. To what extent was the growth of the Ku Klux Klan in the 1920s a result of increasing concerns over immigration?

16. To what extent was the Depression of the 1930s the result of the economic boom of the 1920s?

17. How far were improvements in the lives of black Americans by 1968 due to the Civil Rights movement?

Russia

18. "In the period before 1905, opposition groups had little chance of mounting an effective challenge to the authority of the Tsarist state." How accurate is this statement?

19. To what extent was the outbreak of revolution in 1905 due to Russia's social and economic problems?

20. How important was Russia's military failure in the First World War in causing the collapse of Tsarist authority in 1917?

21. To what extent was the establishment and survival of the Soviet state between 1917 and 1921 due to the weaknesses and divisions of the Bolsheviks' opponents?

[END OF QUESTION PAPER]

X044/302

NATIONAL
QUALIFICATIONS
2008

MONDAY, 26 MAY
10.40 AM – 12.05 PM

HISTORY
HIGHER
Paper 2

Answer questions on only **one** Special Topic.

Take particular care to show clearly the Special Topic chosen. On the **front** of the answer book, **in the top right-hand corner**, write the number of the Special Topic.

You are expected to use background knowledge appropriately in answering source-based questions.

Marks may be deducted for bad spelling and bad punctuation, and for writing that is difficult to read.

Some sources have been adapted or translated.

[BLANK PAGE]

OPTION A: MEDIEVAL HISTORY

SPECIAL TOPIC 1: NORMAN CONQUEST AND EXPANSION 1050–1153

Study the sources below and then answer the questions which follow.

Source A: Duke William's message to Harold before the Battle of Hastings, from *The Deeds of William, Duke of the Normans and King of the English,* written *c.* 1071 by William of Poitiers.

Archbishop Stigand and Earl Godwin, Earl Leofric and Earl Siward, all confirmed by oath and pledge of hands that after Edward's death they would receive me as lord. They also pledged that during their lifetimes, they would never seek in any way to prevent my succession to this country . . . Finally, Edward sent Harold himself to Normandy, that he might swear there in my presence what his father and the other aforesaid magnates had sworn in my absence. On his way to me he fell into the peril of captivity, from which I delivered him by the exercise of both prudence and force. He did homage to me and gave me pledge of hand concerning the English kingdom.

Source B: William of Malmesbury, writing in the early twelfth century, about the Battle of Hastings.

The Normans passed the whole night in confessing their sins, and received the communion of the Lord's body in the morning. Their infantry, with bows and arrows, formed the vanguard, while their cavalry, divided into wings, was placed in the rear. The Duke declared that God would favour his as being the righteous side, and called for his arms. Then the battle commenced on both sides, and was fought with great ardour, neither side giving ground during the greater part of the day.

William gave a signal to his troops to pretend to flee, and withdraw from the field. By means of this trick, the solid ranks of the English opened for the purpose of cutting down the fleeing enemy and thus brought upon itself their swift destruction. For the Normans, facing about, attacked them and compelled them to fly. In this manner, deceived by a stratagem, they met an honourable death; nor indeed were they at all without their own revenge, for, by frequently making a stand, they slaughtered their pursuers in heaps.

Source C: *Kingship and Unity*, G. W. S. Barrow, (1993).

By the end of King David's reign, a vast area of Scotland south of the Forth had been allocated to tenants (almost all newcomers) holding by military service. These men enjoyed the right to transmit their estates to their sons or other heirs by blood or family relationship. Even Moray in the far north was rapidly feudalised. Of even more lasting importance, however, were the burghs which were founded in almost every part of his kingdom outside the essentially highland area. Such an explosion of new ideas, policies and practices could hardly have happened within a single generation without a leader of exceptional energy and determination, backed up by a cohort of like-minded strangers wielding, or protected by, formidable military power.

Source D: *The New Penguin History of Scotland*, R. A. Houston and W. W. J. Knox (ed), 2001.

Scottish society was never fully "feudalised". The kindred-based ethos of pre-existing social patterns in Celtic Scotland blunted the hard edge and binding legalities of feudalism found elsewhere in Christendom. Also, Scottish lordship was strongly regional in nature. Substantial landowners often enjoyed heritable jurisdictions of their domains, which meant that most aspects of justice were the responsibility of the local lord rather than central government. Local justice may, as a result, have been more understanding of regional concerns than the more distant state was.

Source E: from an account of the Domesday Survey, written by Robert, Bishop of Hereford, one of the clergy brought to England by William.

William made a survey of all of England, of the lands in each of the counties. He ordered a survey of the possessions of each of the great lords, their lands, their houses, their men, both bond and free. He sought to know whether they lived in huts, or with their own houses or land: he sought to know the number of ploughs, horses and other animals. In particular, he ordered a survey of the payments due from each and every estate.

After these investigations, others were sent to visit unfamiliar counties to check the first description and to denounce any wrong-doers to the king. And the land was troubled with many calamities arising from the gathering of the royal taxes.

[END OF SOURCES FOR SPECIAL TOPIC 1]

SPECIAL TOPIC 1: NORMAN CONQUEST AND EXPANSION 1050–1153

Answer *all* of the following questions.

Marks

1. How valuable is **Source A** as evidence of the justice of William's claim to the throne of England?
   In reaching a conclusion you should refer to:
   * *the origin and possible purpose of the source;*
   * *the content of the source;*
   * *recalled knowledge.*   **5**

2. How fully does **Source B** explain the Norman victory at Hastings?
   Use the source and recalled knowledge.   **6**

3. Compare the views expressed in **Sources C** and **D** about the development of feudalism in Scotland.
   Compare the content overall and in detail.   **5**

4. To what extent does **Source E** illustrate William's methods of ruling England?
   Use the source and recalled knowledge.   **6**

5. How successful were the Normans in establishing feudalism in England and Scotland?
   *Use **Sources C**, **D** and **E** and recalled knowledge.*   **8**

                                                                               (30)

[END OF QUESTIONS ON SPECIAL TOPIC 1]

SPECIAL TOPIC 2: THE CRUSADES 1096–1204

Study the sources below and then answer the questions which follow.

Source A: An illumination from the 14th Century manuscript, *Les Passages faites Outremer*. In the picture Bishop Adhemar lifts the Holy Lance from its hiding place in the Church of St Peter in Antioch.

Source B: is from *Itinerarium Peregrinorum et Gesta Regis Ricardi*. It discusses the reasons for Philip's departure from the Third Crusade.

When things had thus been arranged after the surrender of Acre, toward the end of the month of July, a rumour circulated all at once through the army that the King of France wished to go home, and earnestly desired to prepare for his journey. How shameful was it for him to leave while the task was unfinished, when his duty was to lead and improve Christian men in the holy Crusade.

However, the French King claimed that illness had been the cause for his pilgrimage and that he had now fulfilled his vow as a Crusader as far as he could. King Richard demanded that the French King take an oath to keep faith and that he promise that he would not knowingly or maliciously trespass on Richard's land or the lands of his followers while Richard remained on Crusade.

How far the French King stood by this agreement and oath is known well enough to everyone. For, as soon as he re-entered his homeland, he stirred up the country and threw Normandy into disorder.

Source C: is from *Lionhearts, Saladin and Richard* by Geoffrey Regan.

Philip Augustus felt he also had reason enough to leave Outremer after the fall of Acre. Apart from the fact that Richard's presence only served to remind him how much he disliked the English king, there was also a major financial incentive to return to France. In the first place the Count of Flanders had died, giving him an opportunity to benefit from the deceased's extensive lands on the borders of France. Furthermore, since Richard was on Crusade and adding daily to his reputation as a Crusader, he would not be able to defend his land in Normandy and Aquitaine should Philip decide to settle any border disputes in his absence. Philip requested leave of absence sending four of his chief noblemen to explain to the Lionheart that ill health made it essential that they return to France . . . Richard was scornful of such an excuse.

Source D: is taken from the Itinerary of Richard I and describes the situation at Ascalon between Richard and the Duke of Burgundy.

After Richard had captured Ascalon, and was carefully rebuilding the walls of the city, a quarrel took place between him and the Duke of Burgundy. The Duke could not pay his men who were near mutiny, and asked Richard for a large sum of money for this purpose. However, on a former occasion, Richard had already lent the French an immense sum of money at Acre, which was to be repaid out of the ransom money from the captives. Therefore King Richard refused his application for money. It was because of this, and other causes of disagreement between the two men, that the Duke left Ascalon; and despite his inability to pay them, the French set out hastily with the Duke towards Acre.

Source E: *The Crusades,* W. B. Bartlett (1999)

Meanwhile, other negotiations had been taking place. Conrad had made his own approaches to Saladin through Reynald of Sidon. Saladin sought the advice of his council, wanting to know whether he should side with Conrad or Richard. They argued that he should support Richard, as he was unlikely to be in Outremer for too long. Saladin's double-dealings soon became public knowledge. Richard's representative, Humphrey of Toron, saw Al-Adil out hunting with Reynald and realised that other discussions were taking place. In addition, the Crusaders in Outremer were as disunited as ever and Richard's envoys were dismayed to discover that Conrad was still talking to Saladin. In particular, the presence of Balian of Ibelin among Conrad's entourage gave cause for concern. If such a prominent man and one much respected by the Franks was openly supporting Conrad, it suggested real problems ahead.

[END OF SOURCES FOR SPECIAL TOPIC 2]

SPECIAL TOPIC 2: THE CRUSADES 1096–1204

Answer *all* of the following questions.

Marks

1. How useful is **Source A** as evidence of the significance for the Crusaders of the discovery of the Holy Lance?
   In reaching a conclusion you should refer to:
   • *the origin and possible purpose of the source;*
   • *the content of the source;*
   • *recalled knowledge.*   5

2. Compare the views given in **Sources B** and **C** on the departure of Philip Augustus from the Third Crusade.
   Compare the content overall and in detail.   5

3. To what extent does **Source D** illustrate the view that Richard I was a good soldier but a poor diplomat?
   Use the source and recalled knowledge.   6

4. How fully do **Sources B**, **D** and **E** explain the reasons for the failure of the Third Crusade?
   *Use **Sources B**, **D** and **E** and recalled knowledge.*   8

5. How important was the lack of unity among the leaders described in **Source E** in explaining the decline of the crusading ideal?
   Use the source and recalled knowledge.   6

(30)

[END OF QUESTIONS ON SPECIAL TOPIC 2]

OPTION B: EARLY MODERN HISTORY

SPECIAL TOPIC 3: SCOTLAND 1689–1715

Study the sources below and then answer the questions which follow.

Source A: from P. H. Scott, *The Union of Scotland and England* (1979).

The Scottish Parliament turned to measures designed to restore Scottish trade from the effects of a century of neglect and discrimination. In 1695 it passed an Act for a company trading to Africa and the Indies. This was the Company of Scotland, which as the first of its ventures, decided to settle a colony at Darien. William, as King of Scotland, agreed to the Act and signed the Charter of the Company. As King of England, he was obliged to do all he could to sabotage and oppose the efforts of the Company.

When the Darien scheme failed, it was largely due to mismanagement and inadequate preparation. Many asked how a country could succeed when its own Head of State actively opposed its interests.

At this critical moment, when relations between the two countries were as bad as they had ever been, a dynastic accident offered a solution. The last child of Queen Anne died in 1700. In 1701, the English Parliament, without consultation with Scotland, passed the Act of Settlement, passing the succession after Anne to the Electress Sophia of Hanover.

Source B: from the Earl of Seafield's letters.

My reasons for joining with England on good terms were these: that the kingdom of England is a Protestant kingdom and that, therefore, the joining with them was a security for our religion. Secondly, England has trade and other advantages to give us, which no other kingdom could offer. Thirdly, England has freedom and liberty, and joining with them was the best way to secure that to us; and fourthly, I saw no other method for securing peace, the two kingdoms being in the same island, and foreign assistance was both dangerous to ourselves and England. Therefore, I was for the treaty.

Source C: from a petition from Stirling Town Council against the proposed union, 18th November 1706.

We desire that true peace and friendship be always cultivated with our neighbour England, upon just and honourable terms . . . Yet we judge that going into this Treaty will bring a burden of taxation upon this land, which freedom of trade will never repay . . . Scotland would still be under the regulations of the English in the Parliament of Britain, who may if they please discourage the most valuable branches of our trade, if we in any way are seen to interfere with their own. It will ruin our manufactories, our religion, laws and liberties.

As a result, one of the most ancient nations so long and so gloriously defended will be suppressed. Our parliament and all that is dear to us will be extinguished.

Source D: from William Ferguson, *Scotland's Relations with England* (1977).

The Equivalent, indeed, had a major part to play in getting members to favour the treaty . . . Part of it was earmarked to meet arrears of salaries and was later so used . . . It is not really possible to say how much money Queensberry made from the union, so tangled are the accounts, but certainly he obtained much more than the £12,000 sterling Seafield referred to.

The Equivalent was politically useful in other ways. The Squadrone was tricked into supporting the Union by a promise, later broken, that as nominees of the directors of the Company of Scotland, they would be allowed to handle that part of the Equivalent intended to compensate the shareholders.

Source E: from the House of Lords Journal, June 1713.

The Question is put to the House:
That permission be given to bring in a Bill, to end the Union; and for restoring each Kingdom to their Rights and Privileges as they had been at the time when the Union was first passed . . .

That charging Scotland with this Malt Tax, will be a violation of the 14th article of the Treaty of Union; by which it was clearly stated "that Scotland shall not be charged with any Malt Tax during this war;"

We must regard it as unjust, to make that part of the United Kingdom pay any part of this tax.

[END OF SOURCES FOR SPECIAL TOPIC 3]

SPECIAL TOPIC 3: SCOTLAND 1689–1715

Answer *all* of the following questions.

Marks

1. To what extent does **Source A** show the problems which resulted from Scotland sharing the same monarch with England?
Use the source and recalled knowledge.　　**6**

2. Compare the attitudes towards the Union expressed in **Sources B** and **C**.
Compare the content overall and in detail.　　**5**

3. How adequately does **Source D** explain the importance of financial incentives in winning support for the Treaty of Union?
Use the source and recalled knowledge.　　**6**

4. How fully do **Sources A**, **B** and **D** explain why a majority of Scots MPs voted for Union?
*Use **Sources A**, **B** and **D** and recalled knowledge.*　　**8**

5. How useful is **Source E** as evidence of discontent with the Union after 1707?
In reaching a conclusion you should refer to:
* *the origin and possible purpose of the source;*
* *the content of the source;*
* *recalled knowledge.*　　**5**

(30)

[END OF QUESTIONS ON SPECIAL TOPIC 3]

SPECIAL TOPIC 4: THE ATLANTIC SLAVE TRADE

Study the sources below and then answer the questions which follow.

Source A: from David Northrup, *The Atlantic Slave Trade*, (2002)

In the eighteenth century, slavery came under mounting attack by philosophical and religious thinkers as well as by slave rebels. Antislavery societies sprang up in many Western countries. Ironically, it was in Great Britain, whose traders dominated the carrying of slaves across the Atlantic, that the largest and most influential abolitionist movement arose. Led by religious idealists—Quakers, Methodists and evangelical Anglicans—the British abolitionist movement also gained the support of a new industrial middle class, whose members identified slavery with outdated economic ideas. For both moral and economic reasons, these people supported the abolition of the Slave Trade as the first step toward ending slavery.

Source B: from a report issued by the London Abolition Committee, June 1795.

We have to inform our numerous friends, that the hostility which many in this country have shown from the use of West Indian produce, has given so much encouragement to the production and importation of East Indian sugar. We are of the opinion, while the Slave Trade continues, that a clear preference should be given to the East Indian sugar, as well as to all other substitutes for the produce of the West Indian Islands, particularly sugar, rum, cotton, coffee, cocoa and chocolate.

Source C: from a Petition of the merchants of Liverpool to the House of Commons, *c. 1788*.

We regard with real concern the attempts now being made to obtain a total abolition of the African Slave Trade. We humbly pray that our views may be heard against the abolition of this source of wealth. This should take place before the Honourable House shall make a decision upon a point which is so essential to the welfare of Liverpool in particular, and the landed interest of the kingdom in general. In our judgement, abolition must also do harm to the British manufacturers, must ruin the property of the English merchants in the West Indies, reduce the public revenue and damage the maritime strength of Great Britain.

Source D: from Petitions of the West Indian Traders of Bristol, May 1789.

It has been found with great exactness that the African and West India trade makes up at least three fifths of the commerce of the port of Bristol. If Wilberforce's Bill should pass into law, the decline of the trade of Bristol must inevitably follow, with the ruin of thousands . . .

Many of our Master Bakers and bread shops depend chiefly for employment on the great number of ships fitted out in Bristol and from the great number of people to be fed on board these ships during a long voyage. Many of the vessels are fitted out by the local drapers, grocers, tailors, and other tradesmen. A very considerable part of the various manufactures that we, the petitioners, produce are adapted to the African trade and are not saleable in any other market . . .

The welfare of the West Indian Islands, and the commerce and revenue of the United Kingdom so essentially depend on the slave trade being carried on.

Source E: from Peter J. Kitson, *Slavery, Abolition and Emancipation* (1999)

External circumstances were to affect the cause of abolition at home. In 1792 the French Revolution set out on a more extreme and threatening direction. One of the consequences of this was the encouragement of revolutionary expectations in the French colonies. In 1791 the mulattos of St Domingue began a revolt which was followed by a full-scale slave uprising. The effect of these events was to frighten opinion at home concerning any attempts to criticise the present constitutional arrangements. The defenders of the trade in the debates of 1792 repeatedly blamed the St Domingue uprising on the activities of the French and British abolitionists. Many of those who had hitherto supported abolition now became nervous at the turn which events were taking.

[END OF SOURCES FOR SPECIAL TOPIC 4]

SPECIAL TOPIC 4: THE ATLANTIC SLAVE TRADE

Answer *all* of the following questions.

Marks

1. To what extent does **Source A** identify the reasons for the campaign to abolish the Slave Trade?
   Use the source and recalled knowledge.

   6

2. How useful is **Source B** as evidence of the activities of the Abolitionists?
   In reaching a conclusion you should refer to:
   - *the origin and possible purpose of the source;*
   - *the content of the source;*
   - *recalled knowledge.*

   5

3. To what extent does **Source C** illustrate the arguments used by supporters of the Slave Trade?
   Use the source and recalled knowledge.

   6

4. How far do **Sources C** and **D** agree on the likely effects of the abolition of the Slave Trade?
   Compare the content overall and in detail.

   5

5. How fully do **Sources B**, **C** and **E** reflect the issues in the debate over the abolition of the Slave Trade?
   *Use **Sources B**, **C** and **E** and recalled knowledge.*

   8

   (30)

[END OF QUESTIONS ON SPECIAL TOPIC 4]

SPECIAL TOPIC 5: THE AMERICAN REVOLUTION

Study the sources below and then answer the questions which follow.

Source A: from a speech by General Conway in the Parliamentary debate on the Coercive Acts, 1774.

It is my sincere opinion that we are the aggressors and not the colonies. We have irritated and forced laws upon them for these six or seven years past. We have enacted such a variety of laws and new taxes and we have refused to repeal the trifling duty on tea. All these things have served no other purpose but to distress and confuse the colonists. I think the Americans have done no more than every British subject would do, where laws are imposed against their will.

Source B: from a letter by John Adams reflecting on the Boston Tea Party, 1773.

The question is whether the destruction of this tea was necessary. I believe it was—absolutely and indispensably so. The Governor would not allow the tea to be sent back. So there was no other alternative but to destroy it or let it be landed. To let it be landed, would be giving up the principle of taxation by Parliamentary authority, against which the Continent has struggled for 10 years. It would destroy all our efforts for the last 10 years and force us and our descendants forever to accept burdens and indignities, desolation and oppression, poverty and servitude.

Source C: from a letter from a Virginian to a friend in Scotland, January, 1776.

Tears fill my eyes when I think of this once happy land of liberty. All is anarchy and confusion . . . We are all in arms . . . The sound of war echoes from north to south. There are armed men everywhere. May God put a speedy and happy end to this grand and important contest between the mother and her children. The colonies do not wish to be independent; they only deny the right of taxation in Parliament. Our Assemblies would freely grant the King whatever he asks of us, provided Parliament plays no part in the process . . .

Source D: from a letter from George Washington to Marquis de Lafayette, September 1781.

But my dear Marquis, I am distressed beyond expression to know what is become of the Count De Grasse. I fear the English fleet, by occupying the Chesapeake . . . would frustrate all our excellent chances of success in that area.

If the retreat of Lord Cornwallis by water is cut off by the arrival of either of the French fleets, I am confident you will do all in your power to prevent his escape by land. May that great good fortune be reserved for you!

You see how critically important the present moment is. For my own part, I am determined to persist with my present plan, unless some unavoidable and impossible obstacles are thrown in our way.

Source E: from D. Higginbotham and J. R. Pole (eds), *A Companion to the American Revolution*, (2000).

It was a great advantage to Americans to be fighting on their own soil and to be more flexible in their military operations than their opponents. They did not fight a massive guerrilla war, but nonetheless they resorted advantageously at times to winter campaigning and night attacks. They effectively employed backwoods riflemen, light infantry and militia in harassing the British flanks, interrupting communication and supply routes, and raiding isolated posts.

British leaders were increasingly frustrated by waging a war 3,000 miles from home against an armed population spread over enormous stretches of territory. It was disheartening to seize, somewhere along the way, every single American urban centre, including the capital city of Philadelphia, and have nothing to show for it other than the possession of property, for America had no vital strategic centre.

[END OF SOURCES FOR SPECIAL TOPIC 5]

SPECIAL TOPIC 5: THE AMERICAN REVOLUTION

Answer *all* of the following questions.

Marks

1. How accurately does **Source A** identify the causes of the conflict between Britain and her American Colonies?
   Use the source and recalled knowledge.   **6**

2. To what extent does **Source B** agree with the explanation in **Source A** of the actions of the Colonists?
   Compare the content overall and in detail.   **5**

3. How typical is **Source C** of the attitude of the Colonists to Britain by 1776?
   Use the source and recalled knowledge.   **6**

4. How useful is **Source D** as evidence of the importance of foreign help to the Colonists in the War of Independence?
   In reaching a conclusion you should refer to:
   * *the origin and possible purpose of the source;*
   * *the content of the source;*
   * *recalled knowledge.*   **5**

5. How fully do **Sources C**, **D** and **E** explain the reasons for Colonial victory in the war?
   *Use **Sources C**, **D** and **E** and recalled knowledge.*   **8**

   (30)

[END OF QUESTIONS ON SPECIAL TOPIC 5]

OPTION C: LATER MODERN HISTORY

SPECIAL TOPIC 6: PATTERNS OF MIGRATION: SCOTLAND 1830s–1930s

Study the sources below and then answer the questions which follow.

Source A: from G. C. Lewis, *Inquiry into the State of the Irish Poor in Great Britain*, (1836)

In all the towns of England and Scotland where the Irish have settled, they inhabit the cheapest dwellings, and thus they are crowded into the poorest, dampest, dirtiest, most unhealthy parts of the town. An Irish family usually occupies one room, or at most two rooms; and frequently, in addition to their own numbers, they take in a single man or woman, or a widow with children, as lodgers. Altogether, the Irish differ more from the native Scots in their living arrangements than in any other way. They appear to be scarcely aware of the problems arising from the crowding of large numbers into small spaces.

Source B: from a report into Catholic schools in Scotland, by a Government Inspector, 1859.

The evening schools attended by Irish immigrant girls are the salvation of many of them who are exposed to the bad influences in both factories and streets of our large cities. When these night schools are in the hands of the religious teachers then they produce the most satisfactory results. On many a wet evening, I have seen these schoolrooms crowded with factory girls tidily dressed and working hard to improve their prospects in life through education. At the end of the school time, these girls would go to their prayers in the church. I was assured by the priest that many of them attended religious services throughout the week, and were of exemplary character in their lives.

The Catholic Church is attempting to help these poor girls to better themselves in life through education and other means.

Source C: from William Ferguson, *Scotland, 1689 to the Present* (1968).

The developing economy of Scotland proved very attractive to the poverty-stricken Irish. In some ways they were an economic asset, providing a hard-working, mobile force of unskilled labour. Gangs of Irish "navvies" did excellent work in all sorts of construction projects, particularly canal and railway building. They also provided a supply of seasonal labourers.

However, they also acted as cut-price labour in the mines, where they were frequently employed as strike-breakers, and they added to the miseries of the hand-loom weavers by swamping that already overcrowded trade with cheap labour. Economic rivalry gave rise to bitter resentment, especially in the coalfields of Lanarkshire, although seasonal harvesters, both Highland and Lowland, also had grievances about losing work to the Irish workers.

Source D: from M. Harper, *Adventurers and Exiles; The Great Scottish Exodus* (2003).

Scots were attracted overseas for a variety of economic, social and cultural reasons. The promise of independence through land ownership was a powerful attraction, particularly to those whose security and prospects had been reduced by the changes in farming in Scotland. For many, the expected neighbourliness, co-operation and familiarity of an established Scottish settlement were incentives just as important as material gain and the absence of domineering landlords. However, the most effective encouragement to emigrate came undoubtedly from a satisfied emigrant's letter home. For emigrants who lacked overseas contacts, professional emigration agents might influence their decisions.

Source E: extract from a letter written by a Scottish emigrant living in Canada, 1889.

If truth be told, many who come out here live out a miserable existence. The people who live in the town of Red Deer are sleepy, with no "go" in them, and other places are no better, some even worse. In Edmonton, the price of property is very high. Our idea in coming to this country was to take up the free land for farming but everything is so different as to how it is described in the agents' pamphlets.

For instance, we are told that splendid homesteads can be had within a mile or two of the railway for 10 dollars. In plain English, this is a downright lie. The *nearest* homestead land I could get was about 35 miles from the railway, and to get land that was worth having, I had to go about 60 to 80 miles from the town and railway. This is the last place on earth that I would care to remain in.

[END OF SOURCES FOR SPECIAL TOPIC 6]

SPECIAL TOPIC 6: PATTERNS OF MIGRATION: SCOTLAND 1830s–1930s

Answer *all* of the following questions.

Marks

1. How useful is **Source A** as evidence of the living conditions of Irish immigrants in Scotland in the first half of the nineteenth century?
   In reaching a conclusion you should refer to:
   * *the origin and possible purpose of the source;*
   * *the content of the source;*
   * *recalled knowledge.*　　　　　　　　　　　　　　　　　　　5

2. How fully does **Source B** describe the importance of the Catholic Church in the lives of Irish immigrants in Scotland?
   Use the source and recalled knowledge.　　　　　　　　　6

3. Why did anti-Irish feeling develop among native Scots during the period 1830s–1930s?
   Use **Sources A**, **B** and **C** *and recalled knowledge.*　　　8

4. How typical of the experiences of emigrant Scots are the views expressed in **Source E**?
   Use the source and recalled knowledge.　　　　　　　　　6

5. To what extent does the evidence in **Source D** support the views in **Source E** on the experiences of Scottish emigrants overseas?
   Compare the content overall and in detail.　　　　　　　5

(30)

[END OF QUESTIONS ON SPECIAL TOPIC 6]

SPECIAL TOPIC 7: APPEASEMENT AND THE ROAD TO WAR, TO 1939

Study the sources below and then answer the questions which follow.

Source A: from the review by the Chiefs of Staff of British Armed Forces, July 1936, following the remilitarisation of the Rhineland.

Our military backwardness has placed us in a very weak position.

The present situation dictates a policy towards reaching an understanding with Germany. This will postpone the danger of German aggression against any vital interest of ours. It is important that we do this because of the extreme weakness of France, the possibility of an understanding between Germany and Japan and even Italy, and the huge risks to which a direct attack upon Great Britain would expose the Empire.

Source B: from a speech by Winston Churchill in the House of Commons, 14th March, 1938.

The seriousness of the events of March 12th (the German annexation of Austria) should be obvious. Europe is faced with a programme of aggression, calculated and timed, unfolding stage by stage. There is only one choice open, not only to us but to other countries. We can either submit like Austria, or else take effective measures while time remains, to head off the danger. If it cannot be avoided we must cope with it.

If we go on waiting upon events, how much shall we throw away of resources now available for our security and the maintenance of peace? How many friends and possible allies will be lost? Where are we going to be two years from now? The German army will certainly be much larger than the French army. Will all the small nations have left the League of Nations and be looking towards the ever-growing power of the Nazi system, to make the best terms that they can for themselves?

Source C: from a letter from the Conservative MP, Thomas Moore, to the national newspaper, *The Times*, 17th March 1938.

If the Austrian people had not welcomed this union, violence and bloodshed would have occurred. So far, there has been none, and this proves the strong desire of the two nations to bring about the Anschluss of which they have been so long deprived by the leading European powers. Austria now has free markets for her raw materials and manufactured goods but, more important still, she is no longer a source of conflict in international relations.

Let us therefore consider the benefits for Austria and Europe before laying the blame for a development which in the end may prove a decisive factor in European appeasement.

Source D: from the leading article in *The Scotsman* newspaper, 1st October 1938.

All the world is agreed that, but for the determination of the British Prime Minister, Europe would have been plunged into a horrible, soul-destroying war that would have killed millions, laid great cities waste, impoverished the nations, and sown the fresh seeds of bitterness and hostility in international relations. We should be very grateful to the statesmen who have saved Europe from such a calamity.

The statesmen of the Western democracies and of the two leading Fascist states have confronted each other over the abyss of war. But now, there is reason for hope in the remarkable declaration signed yesterday by Mr. Chamberlain and Herr Hitler at Munich.

It is true that Germany has given too many reasons for distrust, and her methods are violent, and her ambitions suspect. But, except on a basis of trust, we cannot remove fear and suspicion from international relations, or even begin to lay the foundations of a lasting world peace. Mr. Chamberlain's method of approach is the only way of progress. May he have the strength and support to carry it on to complete the process.

Source E: from *The Shadow of the Bomber*, U. Biailer, 1980.

The government's preoccupation with aerial warfare, and specifically with the danger of bombing, made it necessary that the highest priority be given to the means required to counter an air attack on Britain. Throughout the long debate on rearmament and strategy during the latter half of the 1930s, many experts argued this would undermine Britain's ability to use land forces in Europe. This debate was not resolved until December 1937. It was then decided that spending on the Army would be calculated on the assumption that British forces would not have to fight a land war in Europe.

[END OF SOURCES FOR SPECIAL TOPIC 7]

SPECIAL TOPIC 7: APPEASEMENT AND THE ROAD TO WAR, TO 1939

Answer *all* of the following questions.

Marks

1. How useful is **Source A** as evidence of British concern following Germany's remilitarisation of the Rhineland in 1936?
   In reaching a conclusion you should refer to:
   * *the origin and possible purpose of the source;*
   * *the content of the source;*
   * *recalled knowledge.*   5

2. How adequately does **Source B** explain the dangers facing Britain after the Anschluss?
   Use the source and recalled knowledge.   6

3. Compare the views on the Anschluss expressed in **Sources B** and **C**.
   Compare the content overall and in detail.   5

4. To what extent do the views expressed in **Source D** reflect British reaction to the Munich Agreement?
   Use the source and recalled knowledge.   6

5. How fully do **Sources A**, **D** and **E** explain why the British government adopted the policy of appeasement?
   *Use **Sources A**, **D** and **E** and recalled knowledge.*   8

(30)

[END OF QUESTIONS ON SPECIAL TOPIC 7]

SPECIAL TOPIC 8: THE ORIGINS AND DEVELOPMENT OF THE COLD WAR 1945–1985

Study the sources below and then answer the questions which follow.

Source A: from an official statement by the Soviet Government, 30 October, 1956.

The course of events has shown that the working people of Hungary correctly raise the question of the necessity of eliminating serious shortcomings in their country.

However, forces of reaction and counter revolution are trying to take advantage of the discontent of part of the working people. They are trying to undermine the foundations of the people's democratic order in Hungary and to restore the old landlord and capitalist order.

The Soviet Government and all the Soviet people deeply regret that the development of events in Hungary has led to bloodshed. On the request of the Hungarian People's Government, the Soviet Government consented to the entry into Budapest of the Soviet Army units to assist the Hungarian People's Army and the Hungarian authorities to establish order in the city.

Source B: from Imry Nagy: Last Message (November 4, 1956).

This fight is the fight for freedom by the Hungarian people against the Russian intervention, and it is possible that I shall only be able to stay at my post for one or two hours. The whole world will see how the Russian armed forces, contrary to all treaties and conventions, are crushing the resistance of the Hungarian people. They will also see how they are kidnapping the Prime Minister of a country which is a Member of the United Nations, taking him from his capital. It cannot be doubted at all that this is the most brutal form of intervention.

I ask that our leaders should turn to all the peoples of the world for help and explain that today it is Hungary and tomorrow, or the day after tomorrow, it will be the turn of other countries. The imperialism of Moscow does not recognise borders, and is only trying to play for time.

Source C: from a pamphlet issued by the German Democratic Republic entitled *"What You Should Know About the Wall"*, issued in 1962.

We no longer wanted to stand by passively and see how doctors, engineers, and skilled workers were persuaded by corrupt and unworthy methods to give up their secure existence in the GDR and work in West Germany or West Berlin. These and other tricks cost the GDR annual losses amounting to 3·5 thousand million marks.

But we prevented something much more important with the Wall—West Berlin could have become the starting point for military conflict. The measures we introduced on 13 August in conjunction with the Warsaw Treaty states have cooled off a number of hotheads in Bonn and Berlin.

Source D: from Paul Kennedy, *The Rise and Fall of the Great Powers* (1988).

In 1955, the USSR was mass-producing a medium-range ballistic missile (the SS-3). By 1957, it had fired an intercontinental ballistic missile over a range of five thousand miles, using the same rocket engine which shot *Sputnik*, the earth's first artificial satellite, into orbit in October of the same year.

Shocked by these Russian advances, and by the implication that both US cities and US bomber forces might be vulnerable to a sudden Soviet strike, Washington committed massive resources to its own intercontinental ballistic missiles in order to close what was predictably termed "the missile gap". But the nuclear arms race was not confined to such systems. From 1960 onward, each side was also developing a wide variety of other weapons.

Source E: from S. J. Ball, *The Cold War: An International History 1947–1991* (1998)

A group set up by President Kennedy concluded that "stronger US actions were needed to assist the Vietnamese against Communism in the South East Asia region". These included expanding the ARVN (Army of the Republic of Vietnam), supplying more US aid and sending US advisers to directly participate in anti-guerrilla warfare . . . At the end of 1961 an American government report concluded: "the United States must decide how it will cope with Khrushchev's 'wars of liberation' which are really wars of guerrilla aggression. This is a new and dangerous Communist technique which bypasses our traditional and military responses." Faced with this supposed threat, Kennedy expanded the numbers of US advisers from 400 to 16,000.

[END OF SOURCES FOR SPECIAL TOPIC 8]

SPECIAL TOPIC 8: THE ORIGINS AND DEVELOPMENT OF THE COLD WAR 1945–1985

Answer *all* of the following questions.

Marks

1. How fully does **Source A** explain the reasons for Soviet intervention in Hungary in 1956?
    Use the source and recalled knowledge. **6**

2. Compare the views on events in Hungary in 1956 expressed in **Sources A** and **B**.
    Compare the content overall and in detail. **5**

3. How useful is **Source C** as evidence of East Germany's reasons for constructing the Berlin Wall in 1961?
    In reaching a conclusion you should refer to:
    *   *the origin and possible purpose of the source;*
    *   *the content of the source;*
    *   *recalled knowledge.* **5**

4. To what extent does **Source D** illustrate the development of the Arms Race?
    Use the source and recalled knowledge. **6**

5. How fully do **Sources C**, **D** and **E** explain the issues which divided the superpowers in the 1950s and 1960s?
    *Use **Sources C**, **D** and **E** and recalled knowledge.* **8**

(30)

[END OF QUESTIONS ON SPECIAL TOPIC 8]

SPECIAL TOPIC 9: IRELAND 1900–1985: A DIVIDED IDENTITY

Study the sources below and then answer the questions which follow.

Source A: John Redmond, addressing an Irish Volunteer Parade in County Wicklow, 20th September 1914.

The duty of the men of Ireland is twofold. Their duty is, at all costs, to defend the shores of Ireland against foreign invasion. More than that, they must ensure that Irish courage proves itself on the battlefield as it has always proved itself in the past.

The interests of Ireland—of the whole of Ireland—are at stake in this war. The war is undertaken in defence of the highest principles of religion and morality and right. It would be a disgrace for ever if young Ireland confined its efforts to remaining at home to defend the shores of Ireland from an unlikely invasion, and failed in its duty of showing the gallantry and courage which has distinguished our race through all its history.

I say to you, therefore, "Go on drilling and making yourselves fit and ready for the work, and then behave like men, not only in Ireland itself, but wherever the firing line extends."

Source B: From an open letter by the Bishop of Limerick, the Most Rev. Dr. O'Dwyer, (November 1915).

It is very probable that these poor Connacht peasants know little or nothing of the meaning of the war. Their blood is not stirred by the memories of German aggression, and they have no burning desire to die for Serbia. They would much prefer to be allowed to till their own potato gardens in peace in Connemara. Their view is that they are not ready to die for England. Why should they? What have they or their ancestors ever got from England that they should die for her? Mr. Redmond will say "A Home Rule Act is on the statute book". But any intelligent Irishman will say "An Illusion of Home Rule" which will never come into operation. This war may be just or unjust, but any fair-minded man will admit that it is England's war, not Ireland's.

Source C: from F. S. L. Lyons, *Ireland since the Famine* (1973).

Two lorry loads of Auxiliaries . . . were slowed down by a trick and as the police climbed down from them they came under heavy fire; only one man survived. The very next day, another ambush only a few miles from Cork city caused more Auxiliaries casualties. That night Auxiliaries and Black and Tans poured in to the town, looting, wrecking, drinking and burning—burning to such effect, indeed, that a large part of the centre of the city was completely destroyed. The fire brigade was deliberately obstructed as they sought to bring the flames under control. The Auxiliaries made their own comment on the affair when they swaggered about the streets of Dublin with burnt corks in their caps.

Source D: from *The Twelve Apostles*, by D. Figgis. The author is describing a meeting with Michael Collins which he attended at the beginning of the Anglo-Irish War, 1919.

Michael Collins rose. As usual, he swept aside all pretences, and said that the announcement to use force had been written by him, and that the decision to make it had been made not by Sinn Fein but by the Irish Volunteers. He spoke more strongly, saying that the sooner fighting was forced and a general state of disorder created, the better it would be for the country. Ireland was likely to get more out of the state of general disorder than from a continuance of the situation as it then stood. The proper people to make decisions of that kind were ready to face the British military, and were resolved to force the issue, and they were not put off by weaklings and cowards. He accepted full responsibility for the announcement. He told the meeting with forceful honesty that he held them in no opinion at all; that, in fact, they were only summoned to confirm that the proper people had decided.

Source E: Joint Statement by Irish bishops, October 1922.

A section of the community, refusing to acknowledge the government set up by the nation, has chosen to attack their own country, as if she were a foreign power. Forgetting, apparently, that a dead nation cannot be free, they have deliberately set out to make our motherland, as far as they could, a heap of ruins. They have wrecked Ireland from end to end, burning and destroying national property of enormous value, breaking roads, bridges and railways, seeking by this blockade to starve the people . . . They carry on what they call a war but which, in the absence of any authority to justify it, is morally only a system of murder and assassination of the National forces. It must not be forgotten that killing in an unjust war is as much murder before God as if there was no war.

[END OF SOURCES FOR SPECIAL TOPIC 9]

SPECIAL TOPIC 9: IRELAND 1900–1985: A DIVIDED IDENTITY

Answer *all* of the following questions.

Marks

1. How useful is **Source A** as evidence of Irish opinion on involvement in the First World War?
   In reaching a conclusion you should refer to:
   - *the origin and possible purpose of the source;*
   - *the content of the source;*
   - *recalled knowledge.*

   5

2. Compare the views expressed in **Sources A** and **B** on Irish support for Britain and the First World War.
   Compare the content overall and in detail.

   5

3. How fully does **Source C** illustrate the methods used by both sides during the Anglo-Irish War?
   Use the source and recalled knowledge.

   6

4. How much support was there at the time for the views expressed by the Irish bishops in **Source E**.
   Use the source and recalled knowledge.

   6

5. How fully do **Sources B, D** and **E** explain the causes of division and conflict in Ireland during the period 1912–1922?
   *Use **Sources B**, **D** and **E** and recalled knowledge.*

   8

   (30)

[END OF QUESTIONS ON SPECIAL TOPIC 9]

[END OF QUESTION PAPER]

[BLANK PAGE]

[BLANK PAGE]

[BLANK PAGE]

[BLANK PAGE]

[BLANK PAGE]

Acknowledgements

Leckie & Leckie is grateful to the copyright holders, as credited, for permission to use their material:

2005
Eltis, David & Walvin, James, The Abolition of the Atlantic Slave Trade: Origins & Effects in Europe, Africa and the Americas. Published 1981 and reprinted by permission of The University of Wisconsin Press (p 10);
Illustrated London News Picture Library for a drawing (p 16);
Punch for a cartoon from 1914 (p 20).

2006
Extract from Essential Histories # 1, The Crusades, by David Nicolle, © Osprey Publishing, www.ospreypublishing.com (p 7);
Mary Evans Picture Library for a magazine cover from 'Illustrazione del Popolo' (9-15 October 1938) taken from Modern History Review (p 17).

2007
Extract from Image and Identity by Broun, Finlay and Lynch (eds.) is reproduced by permission of Birlinn Ltd (www.birlinn.co.uk) (p 8);
Luath Press for an extract from Scots in Canada by Jenni Calder (p 15);
Solo Syndication for the cartoon He only wants to lie down with your lamb by David Low (p 16).

The following companies/individuals have very generously given permission to reproduce their copyright material free of charge:

2005
Taylor & Francis Group plc for an extract from 'The Medieval Foundations of England' by G. O. Sayles (p 4);
Extract from The Debate on the Norman Conquest by M. Chibnall, published by Manchester University Press (p 4);
The Athlone Press for an extract from 'The First Crusade and the Idea of Crusading' by Jonathan Riley-Smith (p 6);
Palgrave Macmillan for an extract from 'The Invention of the Crusades' by Christopher Tyerman (p 7);
John Donald Publishers (Birlinn) Ltd for an extract from 'Andrew Fletcher and the Treaty of the Union' by P.H. Scott (p 8);
Hodder & Stoughton for an extract from 'from Lordship to Patronage' by Rosalind Mitchison (p 8);
Image of a medallion reproduced by courtesy of the Wedgwood Museum Trustees, Barlaston, Staffordshire (p 10);
Pickering & Chatto for an extract from Slavery, Abolition and Emancipation: Volume 2 – The Abolition Debate by Peter J. Kitson (p10);
Eltis, David & Walvin, James for an extract from 'The Abolition of the Atlantic Slave Trade: Origins & Effects in Europe, Africa and the Americas'. Published 1981 and reprinted by permission of The University of Wisconsin Press;
University of Wales Press for an extract from 'Revolution in America' by Peter D.G. Thomas (p 12);
Extract from The American Revolution, A People's History by Ray Raphael, published by Profile Books Limited (p 12);
John Donald Publishers (Birlinn) Ltd for an extract from 'People and Society in Scotland Vol. II, 1830-1914' edited by W. Hamish Fraser and R. J. Morris (p 14);
Routledge for an extract from 'The Irish in Britain' by J.A. Jackson (p 14);
Extract from 'The Dark Valley' by Piers Brendon, published by Secker & Warburg. Reprinted by permission of The Random House Group (p 17);
Rogers, Coleridge & White Ltd for an extract from The Green Flag by Robert Kee (p 18).

2006
Detail from the Bayeux Tapestry reproduced by special permission of the City of Bayeux (p 4);
Tempus Publishing Ltd for an extract from William the Conqueror by D. Bates (p 5);
Bibliotheque Nationale de France for an Illumination from Les Histoiries d'Outremer (p 6);
BBC Worldwide for an extract from 'The Crusades' by Terry Jones and Alan Ereira (p 7);
Extract from 'The Union of Scotland and England' by P. W. J. Riley, published by Manchester University Press (p 8);
Extract from 'The New Penguin History of Scotland' edited by Houston and Knox, 2001. Reproduced by permission of Penguin Books Ltd. (p 8);
Pickering & Chatto for an extract from 'Slavery, Abolition and Emancipation: Volume 2 – The Abolition Debate' by Peter J. Kitson (p10);
Houghton Mifflin Company for an extract from 'Abolitionists Black and White' by Adrian Hastings, taken from 'The Atlantic Slave Trade' edited by D. Northrup (p 11);
Blackwell Publishing for an extract from '"The War for Independence, to Saratoga" by D Higginbotham in A Companion to the American Revolution J. Greene and J. R. Pole (eds.) (p 12);
Taylor & Francis Group Ltd for an extract from 'The Irish in the Victorian City' edited by R. Swift and S. Gilley (p 14);
Scottish Television for an extract from Scotland's Story (p 15);
Extract from 'Appeasement' by Andrew Boxer. Reprinted by permission of HarperCollins Publishers Ltd © Andrew Boxer 1998 (p 16);

Curtis Brown for an extract from a speech in The House of Commons by Winston Churchill (p 16);

Her Majesty's Stationary Office for extracts from a speech by Viscount Astor (p 16) and a speech by John Redmond (p 20) © Crown copyright;

Extract from 'The Rising and After' by F.S.L. Lyons, taken from 'A New History of Ireland', edited by W.E. Vaughan. Reproduced by permission of Oxford University Press (p 20);

The Irish Times for an article from 1 May 1916 (p 20);

Pearson Education for an extract from 'Britain and Ireland: From Home Rule to Independence' by Jeremy Smith (p 21).

2007

The History Press for an extract from 'The Battle of Hastings' by Jim Bradbury, published by Sutton (p 4);

The History Press for an extract from 'Scotland: A History' by Fiona Watson, published by Tempus Publishing (p 5);

The History Press for an extract from 'God Wills It' by W B Bartlett, published by Sutton (p 7);

Keith Brown for an extract from 'Kingdom or Province? Scotland and the Regal Union' (p 8);

The University of North Carolina Press for an extract from 'Slavery, Industrialisation and Abolition' by Eric Williams in The Atlantic Slave Trade, D. Northrup (ed.) (p 10);

Danny McGowan for an extract from 'Scotland, Sectarianism, and the Irish Diaspora' from Frontline Online, the website of the Internationalist Socialist Movement (p 14);

The Penguin Group for an extract from 'Making Friends with Hitler: Lord Londonderry and Britain's Road to War' by Ian Kershaw (p 16);

Gill and Macmillan for an extract from 'Green against Green: The Irish Civil War' by M Hopkinson (p 21).